ALSO BY MARK HANSEN

Best of the Black Pot: Must-Have Dutch Oven Favorites

Black Pot for Beginners: Sure-Fire Methods to Get a Great Dutch Oven Dish Every Time

Around the World in a Dutch Oven

Dutch Oven Bread

STOP DROP AND COOK

EVERYDAY DUTCH OVEN COOKING WITH FOOD STORAGE

STOP DROP AND COOK

EVERYDAY DUTCH OVEN COOKING WITH FOOD STORAGE

MARK HANSEN

HOBBLE CREEK PRESS
AN IMPRINT OF CEDAR FORT, INC.
SPRINGVILLE, UTAH

ISBN 13: 978-1-4621-1483-2

Published by Hobble Creek Press, an imprint of Cedar Fort, Inc.
2373 W. 700 S., Springville, UT 84663
Distributed by Cedar Fort, Inc., www.cedarfort.com

LIBRARY OF CONGRESS CATALOGING-IN-PUBLICATION DATA

Hansen, Mark (Rulon Mark)
Stop, drop, and cook / Mark Hansen.
pages cm
ISBN 978-1-4621-1483-2 (acid-free paper)
1. Dutch oven cooking. 2. Quick and easy cooking. I. Title.
TX840.D88H373 2015
641.5'89--dc23
2015003391

Cover design by M. Shaun McMurdie
Cover design © 2015 by Lyle Mortimer
Edited and typeset by Melissa J. Caldwell

Printed in the United States of America

10 9 8 7 6 5 4 3 2 1

Printed on acid-free paper

CONTENTS

INTRODUCTION

Welcome to the Madness!

I'VE BEEN blogging about Dutch oven cooking (at http://marksblack-pot.com) for about eight years now, and been cooking at gatherings and judging competitions. In the process, I've managed to meet a lot of really cool people. I'd like to tell you a quick story about one of them.

One day, a few years ago, as I was surfing the 'Net, looking for more Dutch oven sites and recipes, I came across a new blog called Dutch Oven Madness (http://dutchovenmadness.blogspot.com/). The lady who was doing the blogging had set herself up with a challenge to learn to use her Dutch ovens by cooking every evening meal in them—outdoors and using coals—for an entire year. She would then blog the recipes.

I was intrigued. I just did my cooking on Sundays, so it would be really interesting to see someone do it daily.

Well, day by day, week after week, she went, posting more and more recipes. It was fascinating to read about which ones her family liked and which ones they didn't so much. It was really fun to vicariously live her challenge. During that year, I also got to meet her face-to-face at some Dutch oven activities, which was wonderful.

Well, she finished the year, and her blog continued, though not daily.

Now, here's where we get to the point of the story: A few months after she finished her year-long challenge, her stove died. Suddenly, she could no longer cook in her kitchen. Now, imagine if that happened to you! I think most people would be in a panic. That stove would be replaced quickly! Well, I don't know her circumstances, but she said that it would be a long time before they would be able to afford a new stove.

However, she was able to continue cooking for her family, because she was prepared. She knew how to use her Dutch ovens, and had developed confidence in them. She was still able to feed her family.

Now, I've never had to face that kind of a challenge. But with my skills with a Dutch oven, I know that in the event of an extended blackout or some other local emergency, I can feed my family well.

There are lots of different kinds of emergencies. There are personal emergencies, where the family breadwinner loses a job or is sick and can't work. There are natural disasters, like floods and tornadoes. There are long-term emergencies and short, immediate crises. It's tricky to prepare for it all.

An important part of any food storage plan is a way to cook and prepare all that shelf-stable food you've been storing. There are lots of ways to do this: on a grill, with a solar oven, with small hiking stoves.

The Dutch oven works well because it's flexible and adaptable. It can be used with different fuels and heat sources and can cook a wide variety of things. They are heavy, though, making them difficult to transport, but that also makes them durable. Their simplicity makes them reliable as well.

First, let's talk a little bit about Dutch ovens: how to buy one, how to prepare and care for it, and what accessories you might need. Then, we'll talk a little bit about food storage, and, finally, we'll get to the recipes and how to cook with it! Even though there are some tips to acquiring and using food storage, this book is more about cooking it than gathering it.

Another one of my books is called *The Black Pot for Beginners* and it covers much of the information here, plus more detail. It's a great book for learning how to cook in a Dutch oven. We'll just cover some basics here.

How to Shop for a Dutch Oven

If you're going to cook in a Dutch oven, of course, you'll need to have one. This alone can be an intimidating proposition. Don't be overwhelmed by it. Really, you can cook in any Dutch oven. Read on, and you'll make a smarter first purchase.

There are four basic variables that you'll want to consider when you're deciding which kind to buy: the type, the size, the material, and the quality.

THE TYPE

You have two basic options here: "camp" Dutch ovens, or "stove" Dutch ovens. Which you choose will depend on what you're going to do with it.

A "camp" Dutch oven is primarily designed for outdoor cooking using wood coals or charcoal briquettes. It's got a lip around the perimeter of the lid that keeps the coals on the lid and prevents ash from falling down into the food when you lift it. It's also got legs on the bottom that elevate the Dutch oven above any coals you want to put underneath.

A "stove" Dutch oven is designed primarily for use indoors, in a conventional oven or on your stove top. It doesn't have legs because you're setting it in your oven or resting it directly on your stove's burner. It doesn't have the lip around the lid because there are no coals to be put on top. Some of these will even be coated in colored enamels.

It *is* possible to use a camp Dutch oven indoors, but it's not as convenient. It's possible to use a stove Dutch oven outdoors, but it's tricky.

THE SIZE

Dutch ovens are primarily measured by diameter and sometimes by quart capacity. Common sizes are 10 and 12 inches. You can buy them as small as 5 inches or as large as 22 inches (which take considerable effort to lift, even without food in them). Which one you end up buying will depend largely on who you'll be cooking for. If you're cooking for yourself, or you have a small family, you won't want a big one. If you have a larger family, or if you're thinking you'll end up cooking for groups of friends, you'll want a bigger one.

If this is your first oven, and you're just interested in experimenting a little, I'd recommend a 12-inch shallow oven. This will have the capacity to feed a family of four with some leftovers, and can easily cook for a gathering of as many as eight, depending on what you're cooking. Breads, stews, chilis, desserts, and even small roasts can easily be done in a 12-inch Dutch oven.

Larger and smaller ovens will come in handy in more specialized situations. For example, I use my 14-inch ovens to cook turkeys and larger specialty meats. My 8-inch Dutch oven I use for sides, like rice or sauces. In the recipes in this book, I often use the 8-inch to heat water for reconstituting dehydrated foods.

THE MATERIAL

There are two basic materials used to make Dutch ovens: cast iron and aluminum. There are advantages and disadvantages to both. Even though all of my Dutch ovens are cast iron, I've seen chefs that swear by either type.

Cast iron is probably the most popular. It's the historic choice. It heats evenly (if slowly), and it holds the heat very well, so your food stays warm in it, even after it's "done" cooking. It can take a lot of heat without damage too. Unfortunately, it's also very heavy, and the bigger the oven, the heavier. Cast iron has to be seasoned to be used effectively, but with regular use that seasoning patina gets better and better, and it becomes nonstick. Cast iron also lasts forever.

Aluminum Dutch ovens are much lighter than cast iron, so it's often the pot of choice for campers, river runners, and backpackers that carry their gear into their campsites. It won't rust, so you don't need to season it. It heats up quickly, but that also means that it cools quickly, and it's prone to developing hot spots.

Some say that cast iron–cooked food tastes better, but I've tasted delicious food from both kinds.

THE QUALITY

The best Dutch ovens I've ever seen come from two companies: Lodge and Camp Chef. There are lots of littler brands, like Texsport and a few that are even no-name. You can often come across Dutch ovens at yard sales and antique stores. Some Dutch oven chefs I know will swear by one brand or another. While it's true that there are some that are better made, keep in mind that our pioneer ancestors cooked successfully in Dutch ovens made hundreds of years before modern companies were formed and contemporary casting procedures were invented. I've cooked delicious meals in off-brand Dutch ovens. I prefer my Lodge, but you can be successful with anything.

Here are some hints to check on with the quality:

First, check to see that the lid fits well. Press down on the lip of the lid all the way around. If you find a spot where the lid rocks back and forth, that's a sign of a poorly fitting lid. That will let moisture escape when you're cooking. Again, you can still cook well in that pot, but it won't be quite as effective.

Some off-brands will use different alloys or different sources for their cast iron stock. That can make for variations in the thickness of the pot, as well as the density of the metal. In either case, that can make for more uneven heating and hot spots. Unfortunately, you can't really check for that in the store. It's one reason why you might want to go with a more respected brand.

Still, my forefathers that crossed the plains didn't have a Lodge or a Camp Chef and they survived.

SEASONING

I should add a note or two about seasoning and how that impacts your purchase as well. The seasoning is the black coating of burned-on oils that gives the Dutch oven its characteristic blackness. It keeps the Dutch oven from rusting, it helps transfer the heat to the food, and it also builds up, over time, to be an amazing nonstick surface—as good as Teflon!

Most of the major brands of manufacturers (and many of the off-brands and no-names as well) now sell all of their Dutch ovens pre-seasoned. This makes it much more convenient for you, the beginner. That's one less step between you and your first successful dish.

You might, however, acquire an oven from an older stock and it might need to be seasoned. If so, it will look silver instead of black. You might pick up an old Dutch oven at a yard sale or as a castoff from a family member or friend. It might need to be reseasoned. If either of these are the case, it's easy to learn how to do it.

Summing It Up

Okay, so this is really a 75-dollar answer to a 10-dollar question. What Dutch oven should I buy? My recommendation is that if you're wanting to get started in outdoor Dutch oven cooking, get a 12-inch shallow, pre-seasoned Lodge or Camp Chef Dutch oven. You'll possibly notice that almost all of the recipes in my blog and in this book use that basic size. My two 12-inch-ers are the workhorses of my cast iron collection.

Whatever you end up buying, now you have some knowledge to help you make a wise choice, either to get started, or to expand once you've gotten a few recipes down!

Dutch Oven Size Guide

Size	Uses and Comments
8-inch	When I first got my 8-inch, I didn't think I'd use it much, but I was wrong. I use it a lot for rice, veggies, and other sides. I also use it a lot for sauces and gravies.
10-inch	I don't use my 10-inch much, but it really comes in handy when I'm cooking something and I don't need as much of it. It's great for breads, cakes, and side dishes.
12-inch shallow	This is the workhorse of my collection. I use them every week. Yes, I said "them." That means that I have more than one! You can make almost ANYTHING in this basic Dutch oven.
12-inch deep	For those rare occasions when a whole chicken or roast won't fit in a basic 12-inch shallow, it's nice to have a deep one. If you're cooking a stew or chili for lots of people, you can't beat it.
14-inch shallow	I don't own one of these, and I've only encountered two or three dishes where I really wanted one. I think it would be useful when cooking main dishes for crowds.
14-inch deep	I have two of these, and I use them a lot, for turkeys and hams, especially. Our family holidays would not be the same without them.
Larger	There are other larger sizes and shapes of Dutch ovens. I've not felt a compelling urge to be found in Guinness for owning the biggest Dutch oven of all. I would probably also be there for the man with the most pulled and/or strained muscles at a single time.

Here is my recommendation for a good basic set of Dutch ovens for family cooking:

1x 8-inch Dutch oven

1x 10-inch shallow Dutch oven

1x 12-inch shallow Dutch oven

1x 12-inch deep Dutch oven

This will allow you to cook ALMOST ANYTHING you want to. You'll also be able to facilitate cooking multiple things at once. You can use the deep 12-inch as if it were a shallow one. This small collection also won't cost you an arm and a leg.

As you are able, add these to your collection:

1x 12-inch shallow Dutch oven (a second one, for more mealtime flexibility)

1x 14-inch deep Dutch oven (for holiday turkeys and serving lots of people)

As you become more proficient at Dutch oven cooking, and as more of your family and friends become aware of your burgeoning skills, you may find people coming up to you and saying, "I have an old Dutch oven that I never use. It's been out in my garage for years, and it's probably pure rust by now." Then they may ask, "Do you want it? I mean, you'd probably actually use the thing . . ."

See, I don't care how dirty or rusted a Dutch oven is. That can be fixed. It can be reseasoned.

A little under half of the pieces in my collection now are ones that have come to me through the generosity of others. And the ovens they've given me have come to a good home! I use them all a lot. They are appreciated here. And I always invite the giver over for dinner a few times too, and show him or her what I've been cooking in "their" pot!

Seasoning the Dutch Oven

You'll hear a lot of talk in this book and among Dutch oven chefs about "seasoning" and "patina." These are really about the same thing: that deep, rich black coating that builds up on a Dutch oven over time. It keeps the iron from rusting, and keeps the food from sticking. The patina is made from carbonized oils. The heat bakes layer after layer of carbonized oil into the pores of the iron. I've also read that it makes for better heat transfer from the pot to the food.

As I mentioned before, most Dutch ovens are seasoned in the factory, but there are many brands that are still sold unseasoned, and you may also manage to acquire an old oven that needs reseasoning. From time to time, I'll reseason mine as well, as needed.

First of all, the Dutch oven needs to be prepared. If it's newly bought, unseasoned, it will probably be coated with a layer of wax to keep it from rusting. This can be scrubbed off using hot tap water.

If this is a rescued piece, it might have to be scrubbed more intensely. You might have heard not to clean your Dutch oven using metal scrapers, scrubbers, or harsh detergents, because that will take off the patina. At this point, you can use any of those, because the whole point is to take off any of the old patina, and any rust that might be there as well.

There are lots of ways to season cast iron. You're going to be heating up oil until it literally burns onto the surface of the metal, so there's going to be smoke. For that reason, I like to do it outdoors in my gas grill. It can be done in an inside oven, but when you do, open all the windows.

I start by firing up my grill and removing the upper level grill racks to make room for the Dutch ovens. I have a thermometer on the lid of my grill, so it's easy to track the temperature (assuming it's accurate). My goal is to heat it up to 400°F. More about that later. I put the pot part of the Dutch oven, upside down, without the lid, on the grill. The lid I set on the legs of the upturned pot. I just let them heat up, with the grill lid down to trap the heat.

When they're at 350°F, climbing up to 400°F, I pull the Dutch oven off the grill (using thick leather gloves). I spread a layer of shortening over it, inside and out, lid and legs and all. It's very tricky putting on the grease, because the pots are very hot. If I'm not careful, I can end up touching the pot a little and getting zinged. This happens especially if the melted shortening soaks through the paper towel or cloth I'm using to spread it. It's best to keep the gloves on!

Once they're coated, I put the pots back on the grill the same way as they'd been heating up, and close the lid again.

After about 20 minutes, I open one up and the pot has a smooth, night-black patina on it. Then I turn off the gas and leave the lid open for the pot to cool a just little. After a few minutes, while it's still hot, I pull it off the grill and coat it again in another thin layer of shortening.

Then I leave it on the back porch to fully cool. There may be times when you could do a second coating, but I find that one coating gets it started. Then, use your Dutch oven a lot, and it will build up again over time.

Accessories

A few things are absolute necessities to have for Dutch oven cooking, while some tools and gizmos are really nice to have, but aren't really needed. Let's talk about some of those.

THE LID LIFTER

The whole point of Dutch oven cooking is to get the Dutch oven really hot to cook up the food. So you'll want to have some ways to handle the Dutch oven without actually handling it. The best tool in your kit for this will be a lid lifter.

There are commercial lid lifters made by companies all over, and they basically come down to two types: the Mair style and the hook style. The hook is the most common and the simplest. It's just a metal bar bent into a hook. Some of these also include a T-cross bar welded on. This helps to stabilize the lid as you're lifting it so that you don't tip coal ash into your food. Some people refer to this as "campfire pepper" and just get on with it. I prefer to minimize it as much as possible, as I like the taste of real pepper much better.

In recent years, a brand named Mair has come along with a really great design for a lid lifter. It hooks under the lid loop, like the hook-style, but it has a clamp-like motion with three legs that grip the lid tight. This makes it even more stable and even less likely to shake the ash in. You can lift the lid without tipping it.

Now, I've used both of these, and I think they both work well. You can buy either one in a variety of lengths. Using the longer ones means that you don't have to bend down as far to get the lid off, and using the shorter ones means that your hands are a lot closer to the heat of the coals. I think the mid-range lengths are the most useful, overall. Speaking for myself, I kind of prefer the stability of the Mair-style lifters.

However . . .

I've also seen people, in the absence of anything fancy, use a pair of pliers or vice-grips, or even a hammer hook. It's kind of amazing what you can use if you're clever and resourceful. You don't have to spend a lot of money.

When the dinner is all cooked and done, any of these options can also be used with the wire bail on a Dutch oven to lift and carry the oven to the hungry masses you're wanting to feed. The wire bails are also close to the coals and get very hot as well.

THE CHARCOAL TONGS

You'll be shifting red-hot glowing coals from your burning stack and putting them under and on top of your Dutch oven.

Get some longer food tongs (about a foot and a half, at least), with some kind of spring-opening action. This will allow you to grab as many as two or three burning coals at a time and move them to exactly where you want them. Once they're on the Dutch oven, or the cooking surface, you can push them around with the tongs as well, for even more exact placement. I like my tongs a bit longer, because that keeps my hands far away from the radiant heat of a stack of burning coals, which can get more intense than you might think.

IMPORTANT NOTE: Once you begin using a set of tongs for moving coals, *do not* use it to move, stir, or handle food in any way. The tongs will get gunky and coated with lots of the burned and unburned chemicals that the charcoal briquettes carry. Have a separate set if you're going to be touching food. By the way, I like the shorter handled ones for food moving.

THE CHARCOAL

This is the core of cooking, because it's the fundamental heat source. Some people will use wood from a campfire to cook their Dutch oven meals. While people have been doing that for centuries and were able to cook meals that helped them live another day, it can be more difficult for a beginner to regulate the heat that way. For that reason, I recommend cooking with charcoal briquettes. It really is a more common practice in the Dutch oven world.

Which brand should you buy? Well, I've tried many different brands and some different styles. I think it's most important to be consistent. Anything that burns will give you heat. But different brands and types will burn differently.

Some coal brands will light quickly, burn fast, and then fade and go out. Others will light, take a while to fully catch, and then suddenly get very hot. I like it when coals burn more steadily. They light and may even take a few more minutes to get white, but then will burn pretty long and steady before gradually dying out.

You can use any brand and type of charcoal as long as you're used to and expecting the kind of burning curve it will deliver. You'll know how long they burn, when you'll have to replenish, and when they're going to be burning at their hottest. The last thing you want, especially in the middle of a tricky dish, is to have your coals go out or have them unexpectedly hit their hot peak.

Here are a few other things that I don't use:

Instant light charcoal—It has been already steeped in an accelerant, so you don't need to use any lighter fluid or paper. These tend to have a pretty hot and fast-burning curve and need replenishing more frequently. I've seen meals almost ruined because the coals gave out before the dish was cooked with these. If you know what kind of curve you're up against, however, you can plan for it and make it work. Also, I've seen people add a few instant light briquettes to the stack when lighting their fires, and it helps to start regular briquettes faster. Especially if they're on the bottom of the stack.

Hickory or mesquite or any briquettes that are intermingled with any of the "flavor" woods—These may be great for grilling or smoking, but when you put them under or on top of a Dutch oven, the flavored smoke won't get through the cast iron to the food.

My brand is good, reliable, steady-burning, normal Kingsfords. You can use what you like.

THE COOKING SPACE

The last thing to consider is where you're going to cook. By that, I mean two things: First, where within your space (like your yard, your patio, your campground, and so on) would you like your cook space to be? Second, what actual surface will you be using for the coals and the Dutch ovens to rest on?

When I first began Dutch ovening, I'd heard that hot coals are bad for concrete. It turns out that this is only partially true. A big stack of coals can get very, very hot at the core. Since concrete doesn't conduct heat very well, the surface of the concrete where the coals are resting on can get very hot and expand significantly. Under the surface, the remaining concrete doesn't transfer the heat as well, so it doesn't expand as much. As a result, the surface can crack, chip, and flake away.

As it turns out, occasionally cooking with a ring of coals that aren't packed too tightly together (which is how most of your dishes will be) isn't going to hurt your concrete much.

Still, I put a couple of 12-inch × 24-inch × 2-inch concrete pavers side by side and use that for my cooking surface. I made one for the pot and one for the pile of burning coals. I guess I figured that even though the pavers were concrete, if they chipped and broke, it wouldn't be as bad as damaging a poured concrete pad.

Now I have a few small metal tables that I've purchased. Not only do they maintain the heat well, they lift the Dutch ovens up a little bit higher, so I'm not cooking quite so low to the ground. There are some commercially available metal tables made just for Dutch oven cooking.

For your first dish, don't go out and spend a lot of money on fancier tools and tables. Spend a little time cooking and see what you like and how it works for you. Then you can get the right kind of accessories.

Frankly, if you've got a spot of hard-packed dirt, with no grass, that's fine to cook on. I wouldn't use a spot where the dirt is soft, because the weight of the Dutch oven and the food can make the small feet sink into the earth. Then the coals would be very close to the bottom of the Dutch oven and it could cause hot spots and uneven cooking.

Can you use a regular charcoal grill? Well, that depends. A typical grill has a space below where you put the coals, and then the grid where you put the food. Usually there's too much distance between the two. To put the coals below and the Dutch oven on the grid would probably put the food too far from the heat source, so you'd need to put more coals below. That would throw off the instructions to get the right amount of heat. The legs on a Dutch oven are there to support the oven above the coals at an optimal distance, close enough to get good heat, far enough away for more even heating.

Can you cook in your garage? That depends on how well-ventilated it is. Sometimes, in bad weather, I've done that. My garage, however, has the large opening for the cars at one end, and a side, walk-through door at the other end. With both of those doors wide open, the breeze can blow through and sweep away the carbon monoxide being put out by the coals. CO, or carbon monoxide, is created when burning is incomplete, when things are smoldering. Charcoals smolder, rather than burn. If that gas is trapped in your garage, it can kill you. It can also get into your house and kill your family.

I much prefer to cook in open spaces where there is lots of fresh air swirling around me. Then it's not an issue.

The simple answer? Get yourself a couple of pavers or put a small square of a solid gauge sheet metal up on some bricks and you'll be good to go. Remember to have one space for your Dutch oven and one space to light up the coals.

THE CHIMNEY

A chimney is a pretty common item to find, and most people are probably familiar with it, especially if they've ever done any charcoal grilling. It's a metal cylinder with holes, particularly at the base, and some sort of mesh or holey metal barrier about a third of the way up on the inside. It will also have some kind of handle structure attached to the side.

The idea is that you can put a few bits of newspaper in the space under the barrier, put some charcoal briquettes in the space above it, and light the newspaper. The flames from the newspaper will light the charcoal, and the rising hot air (flowing through the holes in the base) will carry the heat and flames upward to light the upper coals.

The idea is to light your coals without using the harsh chemical accelerants like lighter fluid.

Now, I've always had some troubles with the ones I've bought. I can't seem to get it to light well. The newspaper burns away, and the coals still aren't lit. So I still end up using lighter fluid. I've heard a few suggestions to make it work better.

One suggestion is to liberally drizzle the newspaper with some cooking oil. I'm told that will make the paper burn longer. Another idea is to keep some instant light charcoal on hand and to put a few briquettes of it at the bottom of your chimney first.

I also suspect that if there are holes up the side of your chimney, it will have better ventilation.

There are a couple of things I do like about the chimney, and that's why I use one anyway. It holds the heat in a nice column, so the coals get white a bit quicker. It makes it a great way to keep fresh coals going. I simply keep a few burning coals in the bottom of the chimney, add a dozen or so fresh coals, and mix them up, and in fifteen minutes or so, I have more coals to replenish my Dutch ovens.

I've also developed a cool method of shaking the chimney so as to rotate the coals, allowing more even burning. It has a flick of the wrist when I shake the chimney upward, tossing the coals forward to back, and turning over the entire column of coals.

THE GLOVES

Heavy gloves are useful when handling hot things. It can make it convenient when lifting a Dutch oven, or trying to empty it out. Simple hot pads can work too, but having the protection actually *on* your hands means that you don't have to worry about it slipping. There are several Dutch oven companies that make heavy leather gloves, and you can find them in hardware stores all over as well.

Dutch ovens, like all kinds of cooking, are all about applying heat to food. A major part of good cooking is learning how to apply the right amount of heat at the right time. Too much and you'll burn the outside while the interior of the food is still raw. Not enough heat, and it will take forever to cook and have the wrong texture.

In the recipes in this book, I'll include how many coals to use. If you're using a recipe from another source, one that might not be a Dutch oven book, it might tell you temperatures instead of coal counts.

There are a number of very popular methods for determining the heat needed for a Dutch oven. They vary in terms of accuracy and detail, but all are effective.

The Doubling Method

This is the simplest, the easiest to remember, and the least precise. It's based on the assumption that 90 percent of all Dutch oven dishes should be cooked at an internal oven temperature of about 325°F. It's also based on the assumption that 90 percent of all Dutch oven dishes require more topside heat than bottomside heat. To get to this in an approximate way, begin with the number of the diameter of the Dutch oven lid, in inches. Double that number, and that's the approximate total coals you should use to get that temperature. Then, put about one-third of that total under the Dutch oven, and two-thirds of it on the lid, and that will give you 325°F, once the oven heats up.

For example: I have a 12-inch shallow Dutch oven, so that's going to follow this formula:

12 × 2 = 24 total coals
24/3 = 8 coals below, 16 coals above

If it's a deep Dutch oven, or if it's cold outside, add 3–4 coals to the total, then divide it out. Other variables might come into play as well.

Actually, I recommend using a few more coals, especially when you're starting a dish, just to heat it up quicker, even in the summer. I usually cook more at about 350°F.

Coal Counting Method

In my other books, I came up with this table to help determine how many coals should be used to get what internal temperature. It's more detailed and accurate than any of the other methods, but it's also less flexible as well.

DO size	300°	325°	350°	375°	400°	425°	450°	475°
8"	12–14	13–16	15–18	17–19	18–20	19–21	20–23	21–24
10"	16–18	18–21	20–23	23–25	24–26	25–28	27–30	28–32
12"	19–22	22–25	25–28	27–29	28–32	30–33	33–36	36–40
14"	24–28	27–31	30–33	32–35	35–38	38–41	40–43	43–47

To use the table, simply cross-reference the size of the Dutch oven with the heat required. That will give you the number of total coals to use. Then use the same one-third to two-third split, bottom and top as mentioned above. This is a good reference number, but I don't hold fast to it. Also, I tend to start with a few extra coals anyway.

The Ring Method

There's another, very simple method of setting out the coals that's gaining a lot of popularity. Rather than counting out the coals, you simply create rings of coals. To make a ring, you form a circle with your coals so that each coal is close to its neighbor, even touching. A half ring would be set up the same way, but be missing every other coal.

Smaller Dutch ovens will, by their very nature, have smaller rings. Larger briquettes will have fewer coals in the rings, but their size will compensate.

This system is also less detailed and precise, breaking the cooking process down into four basic heat measurements: Slow (up to about

300°F), Medium (350°F), Hot (400°F), and Very Hot (450°F). In most cases, I've found that you don't need to be any more precise than that, even in baking.

Dutch Oven Size	Slow	Medium	Hot	Very Hot
8"	1/2 ring	3/4 ring	1 1/4 rings	1 1/2 rings
10"	3/4 ring	1 ring	1 1/2 rings	2 rings
12"	1 ring	1 1/2 rings	2 rings	2 1/2 rings
14"	1 1/2 rings	2 rings	2 1/2 rings	3 rings
16"	2 rings	2 1/2 rings	3 rings	3 1/2 rings

The rings in the chart are the amounts for the coals you put above the lid. In all cases, put one ring on the bottom. In long cook times, as coals burn down, move them together, and fill in the empty spaces with new coals.

In all cases, no matter which method you use, when you first set your coals, hold your hand about a foot above the cooking surface, and then again above the Dutch oven and get a good feel for the heat rising off the coals. Learn to feel the heat. Be one with the charcoal, grasshopper . . . ☺

Kinds of Cooking and Coal Placement

Not only will the size of the Dutch oven and the target temperature make a difference, as will the weather, but also the cooking method you're using on a particular dish will have a big impact on your coals and how you place them.

The four basic cooking methods you'll use in Dutch oven cooking are baking, roasting, sautéing, simmering. There are others, and these names will be a bit misleading as well. For example, you'll often use the baking technique for things that aren't really about baking. That method is the most common, so we'll talk about it first.

In the baking method of Dutch oven cooking, you'll have more heat on the top and less on the bottom. Typically this will mean two-thirds of the coals above, and one-third of the coals below. This is so that the air inside the Dutch oven gets heated, and the food is less likely to burn on the bottom. Much of the heat will rise off the top, so there needs to be more coals there. Ninety percent of everything I cook, even though it's not really a "baking" kind of dish, is done this way.

In this method, I place the coals in rings, even if I'm not using the "ring method" to determine how many coals. The underside coals should be just underneath the edge of the Dutch oven so the rising heat from the coals heats the bottom and radiates up the sides. The heat will radiate toward the center. Too many coals in the center can create hot spots. On top, the coals are also placed in a circle, just inside the rim. Extra coals can be placed in a second circle.

The roasting method is for when you want a little more heat on the bottom, with less heat on top. A 50/50 split of coals, top to bottom, is how you set up this cooking method. It's great for meats and long cook times because there's usually some liquid on the bottom to help distribute the heat, so you don't have to worry as much about the food on the bottom burning.

As with the baking method, I also position the coals in a ring.

Sautéing is a bottom heat–only method. You simply put a lot of coals underneath and get the pot very hot. I use this method when I'm pan-searing steaks or cooking fish or chicken as I would on a griddle or a skillet. Usually, when I'm using this method, I have the lid off.

When using the sauté method, placing the coals in rings doesn't work. You have to put them all underneath since there are a lot of coals, and you're only doing bottom heat. One way to do that is to create several rings. It's good to keep a little space between the coals so that air can circulate some. I've seen coals in the center of a bunch like this actually go out because the outer coals were using all of the oxygen!

The Dutch oven will get very hot, and there will be hot spots as well. In most cases, you're stirring up the food, or you're dealing with liquids, so hot spots aren't as big of a deal.

Simmering is just like sautéing, except that you have fewer coals. It isn't as hot, and you usually have the lid on. Even still, there probably won't be any coals on the lid while you're simmering a stew.

Replenishing and Managing Your Heat in Long Cook Times

Sometimes, you'll have to add coals under the simmering stew or chili to keep the heat on. This is a very important part of Dutch oven cooking, because many dishes require longer to cook than the burning time of a single set of coals. It's important to keep the heat fairly steady over a long period of time. To do that, you'll need to keep a side fire going, constantly refreshing it with unlit coals so that you can maintain a supply to add to the diminishing burnouts on the oven.

I've found that the metal cylinder chimneys are great for these side fires.

It's also very useful to have a natural-bristle hand broom that you can use to whisk off ash that coals shed. The ash actually insulates and can keep the full heat from reaching the Dutch oven, and, ultimately, the food.

Plastic-bristle whisk brooms don't work, because the bristles will melt and curl on contact with the hot oven lid.

Cleanup

After everyone is done complimenting you on the absolutely delicious dish you made, it will be time for cleanup. Since you cooked the meal, you have every right to tell everyone else to clean the serving dishes. Even still, you'll want to learn how to clean the Dutch oven. It seems that there are as many different methods of cleaning Dutch ovens as there are chefs.

It's important to clean them right away after eating, so that the food doesn't dry in place. If your Dutch oven is well-seasoned, the food should be easy to clean away. Since I'm usually cooking on my back porch in my daily or weekly cooking, I can clean my ovens in the sink. I just get the water as hot as possible and spray it out with my sink sprayer. Any stubborn chunks can be gotten with a quick scrub with a plastic bristled brush. Don't use metal scratchers or scouring pads here, as they can take off the patina.

Here's another big debate: Detergent or not? I've heard experienced Dutch oveners argue on both sides. Some say that it will take off the patina, others say that mild detergents are fine. Honestly, with a good black coating, I've never found that I needed detergents. The food comes off pretty easily, even cheese and syrups come clean with a little scrubbing.

Whether or not you use detergent, pretty much everyone agrees: DO NOT use your dishwasher to clean your Dutch ovens.

Remember to scrub and rinse the ash dust off the lid and the bottom of the Dutch oven as well.

Once it's been cleaned, wipe it out with a paper towel and let it sit and air-dry for a few minutes. It should be warm from the cooking and the hot water, so it shouldn't take long to dry. At that point, it's ready for storage. Some will say that you should coat it with a thin layer of oil at that point. I used to do that. It was fine for the Dutch ovens that I used week-to-week, but the ones I didn't use as much would sometimes get a nasty smell after a while. The oil would go rancid.

If I'm not at home when the eating is done, there are a couple of options for cleaning. One obvious option is to just pack them away in the car and clean them when I get home. That's what I usually do. Of course, that assumes that I'm going home the same day.

In an emergency, or If you're camping, you'll have to clean it right there. Scrape out as much food as you can with a plastic scraper or wooden spoon. Put some water in the bottom of the Dutch oven and put it back on the remainder of the coals. After it has heated up, use a plastic brush to scrub off any loose bits. Use the water and the brush to rinse off the lid, and then dispose of the water. Again, wipe the Dutch oven out with a paper towel, and let it air-dry.

Storage

At this point, the Dutch oven cleaning is done, and it doesn't really matter so much where you store it. Keep it where it will be dry, of course, and where it won't fall or drop. It can survive the gradual temperature extremes of weather, so a carport or garage is fine. You can keep it in a box, a bag, or out in the open.

The focus of this book is primarily on using the Dutch oven to cook with food storage ingredients. It's not so much focused on acquiring or storing the ingredients. Even still, here are some hints and ideas that can get you started.

Start Storing Food Now

It can be really intimidating to start storing food for your family. There are so many people out there that know so much more than you, and there are lots of people who are more than willing to take your money and sell you their food and their storage system. Which way to turn? What to do?

It turns out that the type of food storage system is less critical. It's important just to get started and to get started today. You don't have to go out and spend hundreds of dollars on supplies and plastic tubs that you'll never know how to use. Just start by picking up a few things at a time.

Look through this book and find one or two recipes that look good to you. Then go out and buy the ingredients. Actually, buy two packages of each ingredient. Then you'll have one to work with and one to store.

Then cook up that dish, and see how your family likes it! Congratulations, you've just started your food storage.

Store What You Use . . .

Most people, when they think of food storage, think of wheat grains and freeze-dried watermelon rinds and other horrors they're not eager to eat. While there are many of these esoteric ingredients that can be made into delicious dishes, it's also a good idea just to store up a lot of the things that you eat anyway.

For example, while you're shopping, and you buy some boxes of mac and cheese, buy a few extra. When you get cans of beans or corn or tuna or chicken, get some extra. Over time, you'll be building up your storage. Then you can begin to get and store some of the staples.

. . . And Use What You Store

Another important part of this is to not just buy food storage and to pack it away, but to actually use it in your day-to-day food prep. Yes, it's good to actually eat this stuff. Not only will it keep the storage fresh as you use it, but then you'll already be accustomed to great food from your storage and it won't be an additional shock when you have an emergency.

Eat and Cook Real Food

A few years ago, I was shopping and I had a moment of realization. One of those flashes of "Ah-hah!" that makes you see things in a new way. I realized that, the more I learned about cooking, the more I liked cooking from scratch. As I walked up and down the aisles of the grocery store, I saw fewer and fewer "ingredients," and more and more "premade foods." I realized that I didn't so much want to buy cans of chili, because I knew I could make a chili that was more flavorful and better for me.

Plus, cooking from scratch will allow for a lot more variety. A can of chilli is always a can of chilli. Beans, on the other hand, can be cooked in a wide variety of dishes, including soups, salads, and even pie.

Manage Your Inventory

Restaurants and warehouses have a concept called "FIFO" to remind them of how to manage the inventory. That means "First In, First Out," or, when you use something from your storage, use items that have been in there a while. This keeps the stock rotating, and ensures that nothing gets too old.

Another inventory concept is that of "par." In business, that's the amount of something that has to be kept on hand to manage daily operations. In other words, a restaurant might say, "we need ten cases of tomatoes a week to manage daily operations." That's their "par" level. So, if they ever get below ten cases, they know to order more, so they never run out.

In home storage, one-half is a good par level. If you get below half your stock of any given item, it's time to buy more.

Don't Buy a Years' Worth of Anything at a Time

There are several reasons for this. First, it's not financial good sense. That much of anything will cost a lot of money, and that's a lot of cash that could be spent on keeping bills current.

Also, if your entire stock of one item ages out at the same time, it will be hard to replace all of that item, whereas if you buy it over time, it will age more steadily.

Finally, if a particular staple is all you have substantially, because that was all you could afford to acquire, you won't be able to do a lot with it. I mean, what do you do if all you have is one hundred pounds of wheat?

Flavorings, Spices, and Condiments Are Vital to Food Storage!

When bought from a bulk supplier, even in smaller quantities, herbs and spices are cheap. It's true that over time they will lose their potency, but that's still measured in years.

A story: One time, my church sponsored a preparedness fair, and at the culmination there was a potluck dinner. Food storage recipes had been handed out, and members of the congregation used them to cook up meals for us all to sample. It was sad to me how bland the dishes were. I was frustrated because I knew there were many people who were discouraged from the storage of food because they were so unimpressed by the flavor. To say "Well, sure, it tastes like cardboard, but it will keep you alive" is to deny how flavorful and wonderful dishes can be with shelf-stable ingredients. And that's where spices and flavorings come in!

Store Water Too

It's very important to store lots of water. My family loves soda. I know, I know, that's horrible, but that does mean that we have two-liter bottles for water storage. You can also buy larger storage vessels, like five-gallon jugs or fifty-five-gallon drums. The idea is to store about one gallon per person per day.

Not only will you use water for cleaning, but you'll also use a lot for cooking. In that cooking, you'll use a lot to reconstitute food that has been dehydrated or freeze-dried. And, of course, you'll want water to just drink.

As you get more and more into your storage, it will be a good idea to have a way to collect and purify water.

It will be next to impossible to store a full year's supply of water for a family. Instead store as much as you can, and use other methods to collect and purify water.

Have a Few Luxury Foods on Hand

On the tail of talking about rich flavors, it's not a sin to save up some fancier things as well as the staples. How about some canned clams? How about some chocolate chips?

Even in the midst of a zombie apocalypse, we'll want to enjoy life a little bit.

Multiple Forms of Food

Each kind of food comes in many different forms. Food comes canned, freeze-dried, dehydrated, pickled, frozen, and in many other forms. In my storage, for example, I keep bags of beans and cans of beans. They work uniquely, and it's good to have them in different forms.

Also, make sure that you have means to access all of the food types. A can opener, for example, is vital.

Store Multiuse Items

Many items that we consider to be food can also serve in other capacities, like using vinegar or lemon juice as cleaners, baking soda for toothpaste, and so on.

Dishes

Also keep in mind that you'll need things to cook in and things to mix in, and measure with, as well as things to serve the food in. Remember to keep dishes in your storage as well. How will you wash the dishes when you're done with them?

Some Thoughts on Meat

Meat is such a big part of most people's diets. That becomes a problem when dealing with things that are shelf-stable when meat, in and of itself, is not.

Meat can be frozen, it's true, and it's a good idea to keep a good supply of frozen meat. In a personal financial emergency, having a good freezer full of chicken, beef, and fish is great. You can thaw them and use them in dishes as is. However, if your electricity is out for more than a day or two, your meat will thaw and spoil.

So, what are some shelf-stable options?

One is to have canned meats on hand. Canned chicken, fish, and ham are more readily available. There are some companies that sell canned beef, but it's not as common to find. Canned meats are nice because the only preparation they require is opening and heating. They're precooked, so you only need to bring them up to temperature.

Another option is to use jerky or other dried meats. If you have your own machines or methods for dehydrating meats, that's a great way to go. Jerky is wonderful because it can be included in dishes as the meat ingredient or it can be eaten as is. In our family, we have a big problem storing jerky for the long term, because we eat it too fast, and none of it is there long enough to keep.

Commercial jerky is very expensive, pound for pound. Most of it comes preflavored as well, which is great for eating, but if you're using it in a dish, you'll have to make sure that the flavors are compatible. Jerky flavors are usually pretty strong too.

When you soak jerky in hot water to reconstitute it, it will soften and swell some, but not to the size it originally was.

Another option is to use freeze-dried meats, commercially available. These reconstitute rather easily in boiling or very hot water, and can be included in dishes that way.

TEXTURED VEGETABLE PROTEIN (TVP)

There are a number of meat substitutes available, the most common of which is TVP. It's made from soybeans and has a lot of protein and fiber. It also provides calcium and magnesium, and (since it's dry) keeps for a very long time. It's very popular among vegetarians as well, since there are no meat by-products or anything similar in it. It is available in a number of flavorings, including chicken, beef, pork, bacon, and unflavored. It's also available with taco seasonings.

While I don't think I'll ever enjoy a TVP steak, if you include it in dishes such as soups, stews, and sauces (like chili or a spaghetti sauce), you might not even realize it's not ground beef. It can be seasoned like sausage and can even be made into patties and burgers.

The recipes in this book that use TVP will include instructions on how to reconstitute it, but the basic idea is to boil up some water and add an equal volume of TVP granules to it. For example, two cups TVP with two cups boiling water. It will absorb the water almost instantly, but let it sit for 10–15 minutes to make sure that all the water is taken in.

WHEAT MEAT (GLUTEN PROTEIN MEAT SUBSTITUTE)

Another option for a meat substitute is to extract the protein gluten from wheat. Gluten forms from wheat flour and is what makes bread fluffy, chewy, and stretchy. You can separate the gluten protein from the rest of the wheat and it forms a spongy, gummy mass that has a texture very much like meat and can be cooked and flavored in similar ways.

It's great for storage in that it can be made from ground wheat grains. Once it's made, it's perishable and doesn't have a long shelf-life, however. In that way, TVP is more immediate and convenient. Still, if you're out of TVP and still have lots of grain, you're in business.

MAKING GLUTEN (WHEAT MEAT)

12-inch Dutch oven with a vegetable steamer
20+ coals below
6 cups whole wheat flour
6 Tbsp. vital wheat gluten (if available)
4 cups lukewarm water

TO START, add the water and the flour in a bowl, and mix it well. Let it sit for a long time to develop the gluten. Whole wheat doesn't naturally develop the gluten as quickly as, say, bread flour, so that's why I suggest adding the vital wheat gluten powder, and letting it sit for a long time. Longer times will make for more gluten development. If you have a way to keep it chilled, but not frozen, I'd suggest letting it sit overnight.

When it's done, put it into a colander or a large strainer and rinse it under running water. The grain solids will wash away and leave only the gluten. It should be medium brown and have a texture like bubble gum. You may need to cut your original dough into halves or thirds and rinse it in batches.

Once it's done, roll all of your gluten together into a single ball.

There are several ways to cook the raw gluten and prepare it for use. I recommend steaming, so it doesn't dry out. Get your 12-inch Dutch oven over some hot coals (see above) with a vegetable steamer in it, folded open. Add a cup or two of water to the Dutch oven, and put the gluten dough in the steamer. If you can, flatten it into a disc. Put the lid on the Dutch oven and let it come to a boil. Once it's boiling, let it steam the gluten blob for about a half hour, or until it becomes more firm.

At that point, you can do a lot of different things with it. It can be ground for soups and tacos; it can be seasoned like sausage. It can be cubed and sautéed, or sliced and seared.

A Few Words about Dairy

Storing milk as a powder is a pretty easy and obvious concept. There are many people, in fact, that drink powdered milk on a regular basis as a way of saving money. It also has less fat, calories, and cholesterol.

It's easy to mix. Simply add the milk powder to the water in a one to three proportion. So, one cup of water, and one-third cup of milk powder. A little over five cups of powder and a gallon of water. When you mix it, stir it thoroughly, and, if possible, chill it for a while.

To make it similar to evaporated milk, change the ration to a two to three proportion. In other words, two-third cup of milk powder to a single cup of water.

To make buttermilk, mix a cup of milk from powder, as above, and add one tablespoon of vinegar or lemon juice. Let it sit for a moment before using it.

Some of the recipes in this book require butter. As much as I love the taste of butter, it doesn't keep long. Fortunately, you have some shelf-stable options. One is to mix it from a powder, using about 1 tablespoon of cool water to each cup of butter powder. You can adjust that for the softness of the butter that the recipe calls for. You don't even always have to hydrate the butter before using it. You can just add in the powder and the water into the overall recipe.

Another option is to "clarify" the butter, making what in Eastern Indian cuisine is called "ghee." If you clarify it, you can keep it at room temperature for a very long time. Clarifying is the process of removing much of the milk solids and leaving the rich butterfat behind.

Now, this can be done outdoors, in a Dutch oven, as described below, or, if you're clever enough to do it before the zombie apocalypse hits and deprives us of electricity or other utilities, you could do it in your kitchen, and then have it on hand when the world ends.

Because this is a Dutch oven cookbook, and because you might need to replenish your supply, I'll describe the process for doing it outdoors.

CLARIFIED BUTTER

I'LL START with just a few lit coals, maybe 7–8, an 8-inch Dutch oven, and a pound of butter. I'll put the Dutch oven on the coals, and the butter in the Dutch oven and let it warm up. You don't want it to get too hot. Just let it slowly melt.

As it melts, the white milk solids will start to rise to the surface, and the water will start to bubble off. Using a slotted spoon, I'll skim the floating stuff off the top, and then let it keep warming. More will come. I'll keep skimming the milk solids away until the remaining butter is yellow and clear. This gets poured out of the Dutch oven into a glass jar and I set it aside to cool, while I add more butter onto the heat and do it all again. I might as well do a few jars at a time, right?

Food Storage Staples

Finally, here is a good list of food storage staples. The first list contains amounts as a good goal for your own purchasing plan. The second is just an extended list of things to consider for your pantry. Many of these things are ingredients in the recipes that follow:

1. 20 pounds of rice
2. 20 pounds of pinto beans
3. 20 cans of vegetables
4. 20 cans of fruit
5. 20 cans of meat
6. 4 pounds oats
7. 2 large jars of peanut butter
8. 2 large jars of powdered drink mix (vitamin C–fortified)
9. 5 pounds of powdered milk
10. 5 pounds of salt
11. 10 pounds of pancake mix
12. 2 pounds of honey and 2 large jars of jam
13. 10 pounds of pasta
14. 10 cans or jars of spaghetti sauce
15. 20 cans of soup or broth
16. 1 large jug of oil
17. spices and condiments
18. 2 large bags of hard candies
19. mini LED flashlight and extra batteries

BAKING AND COOKING STAPLES

- White Flour
- Wheat Flour
- White Sugar
- Cornmeal
- Rolled Oats
- Brown Sugar
- Powdered Sugar
- Baking Soda
- Baking Powder
- Cornstarch
- Salt and Pepper
- Cocoa Powder
- Vanilla
- Almond Extract
- Canola Oil
- Shortening (butter flavored)
- Pasta (all kinds of shapes and sizes)
- Italian bread crumbs

SPICES AND SEASONINGS

- Chicken Bouillon Cubes or Granules
- Beef Bouillon Cubes or Granules
- Yeast (Active Dry)
- Seasoning Salt
- Taco Seasoning
- Steak Seasoning
- Ranch Dressing Mix
- Italian Dressing Mix
- Italian Seasoning
- Garlic (granulated or powder)
- Oregano
- Parsley
- Basil
- Rosemary
- Smoked Paprika
- Cayenne Pepper
- Thyme
- Ginger
- Cumin
- Cinnamon
- Nutmeg
- Dry Mustard
- Soy Sauce
- Vinegar
- Apple Cider Vinegar
- Rice Wine Vinegar
- Lime Juice
- Lemon Juice
- Mayonnaise
- Ketchup
- BBQ Sauce
- Maple Syrup
- Honey

CANNED GOODS

- Corn
- Green Beans

- Stewed Tomatoes (both Mexican and Italian flavored)
- Tomato Sauce
- Tomato Paste
- Cream of Chicken Soup
- Cream of Mushroom Soup
- Tomato Soup
- Chicken Noodle Soup
- Peanut Butter
- Mandarin Oranges
- Pineapple (chunks and crushed)
- Black Beans
- Kidney Beans
- White Beans
- Green Chilis
- Red Enchilada Sauce
- Green Enchilada Sauce
- Salsa
- Spaghetti Sauce

FREEZER STAPLES

- Chicken Breasts (boneless and skinless)
- Chicken Thighs
- Ground Beef
- Pork Loin Roast
- Corn
- Green Beans
- Peas
- Blueberries or Strawberries

LONG TERM STORAGE

- Hard White Winter Wheat
- Dried White Beans
- Dried Black Beans
- Dried Kidney Beans
- Lentils
- White Rice
- Brown Rice
- Steel Cut Oats
- Powdered Eggs
- Powdered Milk
- Dehydrated or Freeze-Dried Veggies and Fruits
- Onions
- Bell Peppers
- Hot Peppers
- Peas
- Celery
- Tomatoes
- Apples
- Strawberries
- Bananas
- Apricots
- TVP (chicken, beef, bacon, taco, or unflavored)

CHAPTER 1

DINNERS AND ENTRÉES

PART OF the challenge of the main dish is to make it hearty and shelf-stable. The perishability of both meats and veggies can make that difficult. Clearly, there are lots of ways around that. There are lots of freeze-dried variations of meats, proteins, and veggies that can be reconstituted and used. TVP can be used for meats, but I find it better if it's not the main focus of a dish. There are many canned meats that can also be used. In the Introduction, there's a section on how to prepare a meat substitute from wheat gluten (page 30). As we approach these recipes, keep in mind all of this substitutability. Be adaptable!

Another thought: Don't be afraid of spices. Suffering through a natural disaster or a zombie apocalypse is no reason to not have flavors. Herbs and spices store well. It's true that they lose potency over time, and that can make a big difference. But old spices won't carry germs that get you sick; they just won't be as strong.

HEARTY ITALIAN SOUP WITH TOMATOES AND SAUSAGE

Here's a great example of how you can take a recipe, work with it, and make it your own. If you follow it exactly as shown, it will taste great. On the other hand, if you're missing one of the veggies or you want to substitute or add in another, it will work out fine. If, for example, you don't have freeze-dried tomato powder but you have cans of tomato paste or tomato sauce, use them and adjust the water to the right consistency. No freeze-dried tomatoes? Use canned diced tomatoes.

TOOLS

12-inch Dutch oven
22+ coals below

INGREDIENTS

6–8 cups water
chicken bullion (if desired)
2 cups tomato powder
3⅓ cups freeze-dried tomatoes

Or, if you're using cans:

about 4 cups water
chicken bullion (if desired)
2 (8-oz.) cans tomato sauce
2–3 (14.5-oz.) cans diced tomatoes

1 cup freeze-dried pork sausage crumbles
½ cup freeze-dried carrots
½ cup dried chopped onions
½ cup freeze-dried zucchini
additional water as needed for soup consistency

2 Tbsp. sugar
Italian seasoning (oregano, basil, parsley)
salt and pepper
garlic powder

1 cup freeze-dried mozzarella cheese

THE FIRST thing to do, if you're going to include the cheese, is to reconstitute it. Cheese reconstitutes best when placed in cold or room temperature water and then left in a fridge or cool spot to chill for several hours or even overnight. So, if you want to include it—it's a delicious addition—plan ahead for that.

Once the time for meal prep is at hand, light up some coals and, when they're hot, pack a lot of them under a 12-inch shallow Dutch oven. If you're feeding a lot of people, by the way, you can easily double this recipe and use a 12-inch deep Dutch oven. Also, you'll want to keep a good side pile of lit coals going, because this may take a while, and you'll want to keep replenishing the coals under your Dutch oven.

Once you've gotten your coals and your Dutch oven set, add the water and cover it so it can start to boil. It can take time to get water boiling in a Dutch oven, especially if there is a lot of water.

When it boils, add the tomato powder or the canned tomatoes. Actually, if you're using the cans, you can just start with the tomatoes in the water and bring it to a boil. In either case, get the tomatoes boiling.

Then it's time to deal with the rest of the veggies and the sausage. You can boil water separately and reconstitute them first, but, hey, this is a soup, right? What's a soup? Boiling water! Just toss them in and let them reconstitute. This will, of course, soak up most of your water, so be ready to add more to keep it to a soup-like consistency. You can adjust it to how you like: runny or thick; soup or stew. Then, adjust the coals, put the lid back on, and bring it back up to a simmer.

Finally, add in the flavorings to taste. I always love making soups with fresh ingredients, but one of the cool things about using dried ingredients is that it infuses the water with the flavors.

As a final touch, add in the cheese, and sprinkle a little more on top as you're serving it.

CHICKEN WITH BERRY SWEET AND SOUR SAUCE

This dish is an example of how shelf-stable can be tasty! This one has a bit of an oriental flavor.

TOOLS

8-inch Dutch oven
10–12 coals underneath

10-inch Dutch oven
14–15 coals underneath

INGREDIENTS

3–4 cups water, for reconstituting

2 cups freeze-dried white chicken chunks, or 2 (12.5-oz.) cans chicken chunks
1 Tbsp. cooking oil
salt, to taste
black pepper, to taste

1¼ cups freeze-dried berries, with a bit of water reserved
2 Tbsp. rice vinegar
1 tsp. ground ginger
1 tsp. soy sauce
1 tsp. dried mint

AFTER LIGHTING the coals, use the 8-inch Dutch oven to boil the water. Using separate bowls, reconstitute the chicken and the berries. Drain the chicken. If you're using canned chicken, of course you won't have to reconstitute it, but you'll still drain off any juices in the can. Season the chicken with the salt and pepper. Let the seasoning seep in while getting the 10-inch Dutch oven heated up with oil.

Once the oil in the Dutch oven is shimmery, toss in the chicken, and let it brown and sear. That'll develop that nice brown tang and a little crispiness.

Meanwhile, drain the berries, but keep a tablespoon or two of the liquid in the bowl. With a fork, mash the berries up a bit, but not too fine. Put the 8-inch Dutch oven back on the coals, and put the berries and the seasonings in to make a thick, chunky sauce. Don't cook it too long.

The chicken, canned or reconstituted, is already cooked, so once it's browned, you can pull it off and serve it with the sauce drizzled over it. I would suggest serving it on a bed of rice.

REFRIED BEAN SOUP

TOOLS

12-inch Dutch oven
20+ coals underneath

INGREDIENTS

4–6 cups water
2 cubes chicken bouillon (or veggie stock for a vegetarian meal)
2 (16-oz.) cans refried beans
½ cup dried chopped onions
½ cup dried chopped celery
2 (14.5-oz.) can diced tomatoes
2 (4.5-oz.) can diced green chiles

salt
pepper
paprika
garlic powder
chili powder

tortillas to serve

ONCE AGAIN, since this is a soup, we're going to be putting all of the coals on the bottom and simmering the ingredients until all the flavors blend.

When there are sufficient hot coals, put your Dutch oven on them and add in the water and the bouillon. I would recommend starting with a little less water and adding more as needed to keep it the right consistency. In the end, you'll be looking for a thick, almost creamy sort of flow rather than a watery soup.

Once the bouillon is dissolved and the water is heated (it doesn't have to be boiling), add in the beans. Break them up and mix them well with the water. Put on the lid and let it come up to a simmer.

Add in the rest of the ingredients. The dried veggies will absorb a lot of water when they reconstitute, but the tomatoes will also provide a lot more fluid. Stand by with some additional water to keep it the right consistency. Add in all of the flavorings to taste.

Let this simmer for quite a while, so all of the flavors combine. Serve it with tortillas or tortilla chips, and, if it's not an emergency, a dollop of sour cream in the middle of the bowl!

SHRIMP FRITTERS WITH SPICY HONEY DRIZZLE

TOOLS

8-inch Dutch oven
10–12 coals below

10-inch Dutch oven
15–18 coals below

INGREDIENTS

1½ cups freeze-dried shrimp, reconstituted and drained or 2 (4-oz.) cans small shrimp
2–3 Tbsp. dried diced green onions, reconstituted and drained
1 tsp. black pepper
1½ cups water
1½ cups flour
1 Tbsp. melted butter
½ tsp. black pepper
2 eggs (freeze-dried whole egg, reconstituted with 4 Tbsp. powder to 6 Tbsp. warm water)
1 Tbsp. freeze-dried egg whites, reconstituted with 2 Tbsp. warm water

2–3 cups canola oil for frying

SPICY HONEY DRIZZLE

⅔ cup honey
2 Tbsp. fresh hot sauce
sea salt to taste

AFTER LIGHTING and heating up the coals, use the 8-inch Dutch oven to heat some water (for reconstituting ingredients), and use the 10-inch Dutch oven to heat the oil. Some thoughts on this: When I first found this recipe, it called for "deep frying" the fritters. Deep frying in a Dutch oven over coals is difficult because it's hard to get sufficient oil up to 350°F using charcoal briquettes. There are ways to do it, but they involve special hardware that will lift the Dutch oven and the coals and allow ventilation underneath. Most folks don't have this.

Instead, I recommend using a smaller Dutch oven (like a 10-inch), and putting less oil in it, and "shallow frying" the food. If you fry food in oil that's not hot enough, not only will it not cook right but it will also absorb more of the oil and end up feeling and tasting greasy. Canola oil is good for frying, by the way, because it has a higher smoking point than, say, olive oil.

So, when you're heating up the oil, put in enough for it to be about ¾-inch to 1-inch deep, and put a lid on the Dutch oven, checking the temperature from time to time.

Reconstitute the ingredients that need it first, then mix the ingredients together. The butter, if it's not mixed from powder, can be melted in the 8-inch Dutch oven.

Drop spoonfuls of the dough into the hot oil. Don't put too many in at once, or the cooking will reduce the temperature of the oil too much. Fry them until they're nicely brown on both sides, drain them, and cool them on paper towels.

Mix the honey with the hot sauce and salt, heat it, and use it as a dip or drizzle.

SWEDISH BEEF AND RICE

This recipe calls for "Golden Mushroom Soup," which is a lot like cream of mushroom soup, except that it's made with beef broth and a bit of tomato. You could substitute the cream soup if you don't have the golden, but it won't taste as rich and beefy.

This could be easily doubled and made in a 12-inch Dutch oven.

TOOLS

8-inch Dutch oven
10–12 coals below

10-inch Dutch oven

15–18 coals below

INGREDIENTS
1½ cups rice
3 cups water

1 (10.5-oz.) can golden mushroom soup
1½ tsp. Worcestershire sauce
4 Tbsp. canned butter, clarified butter, or powdered butter equivalent
1 (12-oz.) can evaporated milk

1½ cups water
¼ cup flour

1 (12-oz.) can roast beef, drained

AFTER GETTING the coals lit and white, put some under the 8-inch Dutch oven, and then put in the rice and water. Put the lid on and watch for it to boil. I can tell it's boiling because I can see steam starting to vent out from under the lid. When this happens, I let it cook, boiling for about 10 minutes, before taking it off the coals. Without removing the lid, I let it sit for at least another 15 to 20 minutes. This is my foolproof way of cooking rice without under or overdoing it.

While all that's happening, you can be cooking the beef. Start by putting the coals under your 10-inch Dutch oven and adding the second set of ingredients (the soup, the sauce, butter, and evaporated milk). Then stir the water and the flour together until it's smooth and add it in. Finally, put in the canned beef.

After it has simmered for a bit, add in any seasonings (to taste) you'd like—salt, pepper, chili. Pour the beef mixture over the rice and serve it up!

CURRIED LENTILS AND RICE

Like the dish above, this is easy to double and make in a 12-inch shallow Dutch oven. This is another great example of using great flavors with relatively shelf-stable ingredients to create a memorable dish!

TOOLS
8-inch Dutch oven
10–12 coals below

10-inch Dutch oven
15–18 coals below

INGREDIENTS
2 cups long-grain white rice
4 cups water

1 Tbsp. vegetable or canola oil
1 Tbsp. curry powder
½ tsp. onion powder

4 cups water
1 cup lentils (red or brown)

1 tsp. honey
1 Tbsp. balsamic vinegar
1 tsp. salt

FIRST, LIGHT up a chimney full of coals and get the rice cooking (see page 44). While that's cooking, work on the curry.

In a lot of Eastern/Indian cooking, the spices are "activated" first by cooking them slightly in oil. The flavors of most herbs and spices are oil soluble, so this infuses the flavors throughout the oil. So, start by heating the oil in the bottom of the 10-inch Dutch oven, over the coals as listed above. Add in the curry and onion powders, and stir for a few minutes. It will start to smell wonderful. If your curry is mild and you want it hotter, add some chili powder.

Then, add in the water and the lentils. Stir, cover, and bring to a boil. Once it's boiling, you can pull some coals until it's just simmering, and that's how you'll want to maintain it for the rest of the cooking.

Once the lentils are soft (about a half hour or so), you can remove it from the heat. Stir in the honey, the balsamic vinegar, and the salt. Serve it over the rice.

CHICKEN PARMESAN

This one is kind of different. It's not purely shelf-stable, though it could be made so. For example, you could use canned chicken breast. But this recipe is more like an example of how your food storage can be used to enhance fresh or frozen meat. I mean, when the zombie apocalypse comes and the world is shutting down, you won't have access to your fridge or freezer. But if the world isn't ending and you just want a little more out of what you've been storing, this is a great one because it's delicious and fancy and wonderful.

And, I guess, if you've been raising your own chickens, you could use one of those . . .

Also, this one has a lot of steps, and it's not quick and easy. I get that. Sometimes, however, even in emergency conditions, it can be good for the soul to eat well. I'm not saying this should go for every meal, but once in a while, it's nice to have something really good.

TOOLS

8-inch Dutch oven (for the sauce)
7–8 coals underneath

10-inch Dutch oven (for the noodles)
18+ coals underneath

12-inch Dutch oven (for the chicken and the final dish)

22+ coals underneath for frying
10–12 coals underneath for baking
14–16 coals above

INGREDIENTS

1 cup of "buttermilk" (add 1 tablespoon of lemon juice or white vinegar for every 1 cup of powdered milk, then let it set for 5–10 minutes.)
3 chicken breasts (or the equivalent in canned chicken)

1 (14.5-oz.) can diced tomatoes
2 (8-oz.) cans tomato sauce
to taste:
garlic powder
salt
pepper
basil

oregano
chili powder (optional)

about 4 cups water
1 (16-oz.) pkg. of spaghetti, linguini, fettuccine, or egg noodles

2 Tbsp. olive oil
2 eggs (2 Tbsp. of powdered eggs + 4 Tbsp. of water)
1 cup of white or wheat flour
¼ cup cornmeal (optional)
salt
pepper
1 tsp. basil
1 tsp. oregano
Parmesan cheese

2 cups mozzarella cheese (fresh or freeze-dried)

IF YOU'RE going to use freeze-dried mozzarella, the first step would be to reconstitute it and let it set (see pages 38–39). The second step is to mix up the milk and use the acid (lemon juice or vinegar) to make it into buttermilk. In a zip-top bag, add the buttermilk to the chicken breasts and set it aside for an hour or more. If you have ice or cold water, it will chill.

Then, when it's cooking time, light up some coals. You'll need quite a lot. This is a three-pot meal.

In the 8-inch Dutch oven, mix the tomatoes, sauce and flavorings to make a marinara sauce and set the Dutch oven on the coals to simmer. The longer the sauce simmers, the richer the flavors will be.

In the 10-inch Dutch oven, pour in the water, cover it, and set it on the coals. Bring it up to a boil, and then add in the pasta, stirring. If you leave the lid off, you'll probably lose the boil, so keep it covered. In 8–10 minutes, check the pasta. If it's cooked, but still resists your teeth a little, it's done. Pull it off and drain it. It can actually be a little underdone, partly because it will continue cooking a bit as it rests, but also because it will bake some with the sauce in the next steps.

Prep the 12-inch Dutch oven by putting lots of coals under it and the oil inside it. Let it heat up so the oil shimmers but doesn't smoke. Mix or beat the eggs in a bowl. Mix the flour and herbs in another bowl. Arrange these bowls near the heated Dutch oven.

There are two ways you can prepare the chicken breasts. You can cut them into strips (I usually do three strips, like fingers, per breast). Alternately, you can pound them flat between two sheets of wrapping plastic or waxed paper. Either method will make for more even cooking. If you're using canned chicken, just break the meat into chunks. Dredge the meat pieces first in the flour mix, then in the egg, and then back in the flour. Then put them in the Dutch oven to fry. Let them frizzle for about 10 minutes, and then flip them over for another 10 minutes or so.

At this point, you might need some fresh coals, so add some to your chimney.

When the chicken is fried, it's time to assemble the final dish. Wipe out the 12-inch Dutch oven, and dump in the pasta as a base. Pour most of the marinara over the noodles. Lay the chicken on top of that. Spoon some of the marinara on top of the chicken pieces, but not too much, lest they get too soggy. Finally, scatter the mozzarella cheese over all of it, along with some more Parmesan cheese, and reset the coals to the baking configuration. All of the ingredients are fully cooked, so we're just blending the flavors, bringing them all up to full temperature, and melting the cheese. About 20 minutes should do it, depending on how brown you like your cheese.

FROM-THE-PANTRY JAMBALAYA

Jambalaya is one of my favorite Cajun dishes, and I love to make it fresh. However, in times of crisis, that's not always an option! With a bit of creativity and some good seasonings, however, you can take shelf-stable and canned ingredients and make it into a delicious substitute.

Another cool thing about jambalaya is that it's so flexible. You can really do a lot of adapting and adjusting based on what you have on hand.

TOOLS
12-inch Dutch oven
10–12 coals below
14–18 coals above

INGREDIENTS

2 (5- to 7-oz.) pkgs. rice mix of any flavor: chicken, beef, creole, or Spanish
1–2 (14-oz.) cans diced tomatoes
1–2 (14-oz.) cans black or red beans, drained and rinsed
1 (14-oz.) can corn, drained
1–2 (4.5-oz.) cans diced green chiles
½ cup dried onions
4 cups water

2–3 (4.5-oz.) cans shrimp, clams, or other seafood
2–3 (12.5-oz.) cans chicken breast or any kind of meat

salt
pepper
garlic powder
chili powder

THIS ONE'S really simple. You start out with some lit coals, and while they're growing white, you drop all the first batch ingredients into your Dutch oven. If you're feeding a smaller crowd, use a 10-inch Dutch oven and use the lower quantities in the ingredients list. Let everything simmer/bake for at least 20–30 minutes, and then begin adding the seasonings listed. If you have some kind of shelf-stable lemon flavoring (like some dried zest), add that in pretty liberally as well. If not, the acidity in the tomatoes can carry the day.

After another half hour or so, the stew should be ready. To be certain, check the rice. If it's still crunchy in the middle, let it cook longer. If you need to, replenish a handful of coals from your side fire, and put 3–4 below and 4–6 more on top.

TUNA NOODLE CASSEROLE

Even though this dish has quite a few steps and requires two Dutch ovens, it's still quite simple. There are not many ingredients, and it's all basically a mix and cook process.

TOOLS

10-inch Dutch oven
16–18 coals below

12-inch Dutch oven
10–12 coals below
16–18 coals above

INGREDIENTS
3–4 cups water
1 (16-oz.) pkg. egg noodles
salt

1 (10.75-oz.) can cream of mushroom soup
1 (15-oz.) can peas, drained
2 (5-oz.) cans tuna, drained
1 (4-oz.) can sliced mushrooms (optional)
¼ cup freeze dried veggies (onion, pepper, celery) (optional)
1 cup milk (3 Tbsp. dry milk + 1 cup water)
salt
pepper
paprika
garlic powder

½ cup bread crumbs

I'LL START with some lit coals and put the 10-inch Dutch oven on with some water to boil. I make sure it's covered so it will boil more quickly. You could use the 12-inch Dutch oven, but don't use so much water that it takes forever to boil.

Once the water is at a nice rolling boil, I add the noodles and let them cook, covered, for 12–15 minutes. I check a noodle by biting it. You want it to be "al dente," meaning that it's not totally soft and resists your teeth a little. If it's still a little tough in the middle, that's good, because it will cook more in the next step.

While boiling and cooking the noodles, I gather the other ingredients. This is pretty simple. I just mix them in the 12-inch Dutch oven. Some of the ingredients, like the veggies or the mushrooms, are optional, but they'll add a lot of flavor and some substance to the whole mix. Otherwise, the soup and the milk can make things a bit runny.

When the pasta is done, I'll either drain it out, or scoop them out with a slotted spoon, and add them into the mixture in the 12-inch Dutch oven. I'll stir that all up and smooth it out so it's level. On top, I'll sprinkle the bread crumbs (or maybe little French onion strings, if you've got them).

When that's all ready, I'll put it out onto the coals, as listed above, and let it bake for 45 minutes or so. Everything is already fully "cooked," so you're just bringing it all up to temperature and blending all the flavors.

When it's all warmed through, serve it straight from the Dutch oven!

CHICKEN TORTELLINI SOUP

There are two ways to make this recipe. One way is a more clear, chicken broth style, and the other way is a tomatoey thing with a bit of a marinara sort of flavor. Either one is great, and there isn't much of a difference in the ingredients or the process.

TOOLS

12-inch Dutch oven
18–20 coals below (to start, less as it simmers)

INGREDIENTS

8 cups water
6 cubes chicken bouillon
1 (12.5-oz.) can of chicken (or use freeze-dried chicken)

¼ cup dehydrated celery
2 Tbsp. dehydrated onions
½–1 tsp. celery seed
½–1 tsp. basil
1 tsp. garlic salt
1 tsp. salt
½–1 tsp. pepper
sprinkle of red pepper flakes (optional)
other dried herbs like parsley or oregano

1 (12-oz.) pkg. dry tortellini

Additional ingredients for the marinara version:
1 (14.5-oz.) can diced tomatoes
1 (6-oz.) can tomato paste

AS WITH all of these dishes, I start with the ceremonial lighting of the coals!

I guess it's not really so ceremonial.

Oh, well . . .

Anyway, once the coals are getting a bit white, I'll put the water in the Dutch oven along with the bouillon cubes and cover it. I'll let it boil to dissolve the cubes. Once that's done, I'll add the chicken and the other ingredients and flavorings in the next set of ingredients, and let that come to a boil again, covered. If you want to do the tomato-ish version, add those ingredients in at this point too.

Finally, when it's boiling again, add in the tortellini and cover it again. Let it simmer for 10–15 minutes, and then serve! If you have some grated Parmesan, that's a nice touch to add.

TWELVE BEAN AND HAM SOUP

Each Christmas, I cook a big bone-in ham in my 14-inch Dutch oven. That's not really food storage, but if you freeze the bone and any extra meat attached to it, you can have a great soup in the next few days. It's a great thing to warm you up from the inside. Another thing I like about it is that it will infuse your soup with the flavorings you used on the ham. This last Christmas, for example, the ham was basted in an orange and brown sugar glaze, so my soup had a tangy and sweet edge.

If you don't do a Christmas ham, maybe someone you know does, and you can use their bone. Or canned ham will work great too.

This will take a while to cook, because beans take a long time. It's definitely worth the wait, though.

TOOLS

12-inch Dutch oven
18–20 coals below (to start, less as it simmers)

INGREDIENTS

1 (16-oz.) 12-bean soup mix
8 cups water (or 4 cups water + 4 cups chicken stock)
1 tsp. salt
1 ham bone (or about 16 oz. canned ham, cubed)

1 chopped onion (can use dehydrated)
3 stalks celery, diced (can use dehydrated)
1 (28-oz.) can whole tomatoes
2 carrots, diced (can use dehydrated)

1 tsp. ginger
4 Tbsp. BBQ sauce
1 Tbsp. sugar
1 small clove garlic
¼ tsp. lemon pepper
2 Tbsp. ketchup
1 pinch red pepper flakes

THIS MEAL actually starts off the night before, when I'll put the beans in a bowl and soak them in water, having at least a couple of inches of water on top of them. This is important to do, because they'll soak up the water and there won't be enough if you only cover the beans.

Another note on the beans themselves: You can buy bags of "12 Bean Soup" that already has 12 different beans in it, or you can just mix it from whatever legumes you have on hand. Eating different kinds of beans is good for you, by the way, because multiple bean types will combine into more complete proteins.

The next day, I'll pour off the excess water, and put the beans, the bone, and the salt in my Dutch oven with 8 cups water. I'll put the Dutch oven lid on and set it on about 20 lit coals. In a while, it will start boiling. From then on, I'll be careful to maintain fresh coals to keep it simmering.

After about an hour, the beans will be either tender or gettin' there. Then, I'll add in the veggies and the seasonings and cook it for another 1–2 hours to infuse the flavors and fully cook all of the beans.

After it's getting close to being done, I'll start tasting it and adding more seasonings or sauces as I think it needs it. Go easy on the sugar (the ketchup and BBQ sauce already have lots in them). I like to add more of each as it's simmering to make the flavors more bold. I don't like bland soups.

DUTCH OVEN SPLIT PEA SOUP WITH HAM

Here's another ham-bone soup that's delicious! Again, if you don't have the ham bone, you can use canned ham. I usually use fresh ingredients like onions, celery, and so on, but dehydrated works great in soups.

TOOLS

12-inch Dutch Oven
15–20 coals below

INGREDIENTS

6 cups water (or 3 cups water + 3 cups chicken stock)
1 (1-lb.) bag dried split peas
1 ham bone with lots of meat left on it, or some canned ham

1 cup dehydrated onion
1 cup dehydrated celery
1 cup dehydrated sweet pepper

Generous shakes of the following:
oregano
parsley
chili powder
garlic powder
salt and coarse ground pepper

THIS ONE doesn't take as long as the Twelve Bean and Ham Soup, because split peas will cook faster than beans and don't have to be soaked overnight.

The process is the same as the Twelve Bean and Ham Soup, otherwise. I start with hot coals, and put the 12-inch Dutch oven on, with the water, the bone, and the peas. I let them come to a boil and simmer for about 45 minutes. Then I add in the other flavorings. The beans will be soft enough to eat soon after, but I like to cook it for at least another 45 minutes to combine the flavors.

Thick soups like split pea serve well in bread bowls or poured over rolls!

NAVY BEAN AND HAM SOUP

Here's a third variation on the bean and ham soup. You know, for my money, you can never have too many soups like this. I love them all.

I looked it up, and, as I suspected, the name *navy bean* comes from the fact that it was a staple of the rations in the US Navy in the 1800s. It turns out that canned versions of these beans don't lose their nutritional value like other beans and veggies do. Good to know!

TOOLS

12-inch Dutch oven
15–20 coals below

INGREDIENTS

5 cups dry white beans
2½ Tbsp. chicken-flavored stock base
8 cups water
1 tsp. salt

⅔ cup dehydrated diced ham (or a ham bone, if you've got it)
2 crumbled bay leaves
½ cup dehydrated minced onions
¼ tsp. ground cloves
½ cup dehydrated minced carrots
½ tsp. pepper
½ tsp. cayenne pepper

THE FIRST step is to soften the beans overnight. I'll put the dried beans in a bowl and drown them in water, at least two inches higher than the beans. I'll let them soak overnight so they'll be ready to cook in the morning.

You could, of course, just use canned white beans. Nothing wrong with that. In that case, they're already cooked and you just want to add them in with everything else and simmer them to share the flavors.

I'll put the Dutch oven onto the heated coals and added the first set of ingredients. I'll let the beans cook, covered, at a boil for about an hour. If I've got a ham bone, I'll include that in the initial boil, but if I'm just adding canned or dehydrated ham, I'll add it in later after the beans are soft.

Once they're soft, I add in the other ingredients and let them simmer. As before, once it's been cooking a while, maybe 45 minutes to an hour (I'll have to maintain a side fire and replenish my coals from time to time), I'll start taste testing my soup and adding flavors as I wish.

Be careful with the cayenne. Add a bit, let it simmer and infuse with the other flavors, and then taste. You can always add more heat, but you can't take it out.

TVP SLOPPY JOE

As one of the available substitutes for fresh meat, TVP really delivers, especially if it's not the main focus of your meal. If it's a part of a stew, or mixed in with lots of other ingredients, it can add substance and texture as well as a meaty flavor.

I've always loved sloppy joes. Personally, I prefer them served open-faced, eaten with a fork, because then I can spread more meat mix onto the bread. I like them as sandwiches, too, but not as much. I'm already a pretty messy eater, and I don't need to be set up for failure right from the start.

TOOLS
10-inch Dutch oven
15–17 coals below

INGREDIENTS
2 cups water

½ cup dehydrated onion
½ cup dehydrated or canned green pepper, diced
1½ cups dry textured vegetable protein (TVP)

2½ cups tomato sauce
1–2 Tbsp. chili powder
1 pinch pepper
1 tsp. salt
1 tsp. soy sauce
1 tsp. mustard
1 tsp. sugar or molasses

Hamburger buns or bread to serve on.

I START with lit coals, and I put them under my 10-inch Dutch oven with the water. I put the lid on and let it come to a boil. Once it's rolling nicely, I'll toss in the dehydrated ingredients from the next set. You might need to add more water if it all gets absorbed. Not too much more, since there will be some additional liquid in ingredients that will be added.

Then I'll add in the tomato sauce and the flavorings. Let it simmer for a bit, covered, and taste it. Some of the flavorings might need an adjustment. Once it's tasting good, let it simmer just a bit longer, maybe a half hour total, and then serve it on hamburger buns or bread!

TVP VEGGIE BURGERS

Honestly, I'm not a big veggie burger fan. I've tasted some that are good, but I'm basically a meat-ivore. Still, if I'm living off storage, I'm not opposed to substitutes like beans or TVP for my proteins. One thing I'll say, most veggie burger recipes include more seasonings than their meat counterparts, so it does end up being much more flavorful, even if the texture is different.

TOOLS

8-inch Dutch oven (for the water)
10–12 coals below

12-inch Dutch oven (for the burgers)
18–20 coals below

INGREDIENTS

2 cups boiling water
1¼ cups textured vegetable protein (TVP)
¼ cup dehydrated carrot
¼ cup dehydrated celery
¼ cup dehydrated onion

2 Tbsp. ketchup

Worcestershire sauce
soy sauce
½ tsp. salt
½ tsp. marjoram

1 tsp. oregano
1 Tbsp. parsley flakes
1 Tbsp. garlic powder
½ cup chopped fresh basil

⅓ cup flour

1–2 Tbsp. oil

FIRST, I'LL light up the coals, as I do with all of the recipes. Once they're glowing, I'll use the 8-inch Dutch oven (lid on) to get the water boiling. You could use the 12-inch oven, but it would require more coals.

Once the water is boiling, I'll pour that into a bowl and add in the rest of the first set of ingredients. I'll let that set and steep for a while. About 10 minutes later, I'll add the ketchup and mix it to a nice pasty consistency, adding more or less ketchup as necessary.

Then, I add in the flavorings in the third set of ingredients and mix it all up. The final step is to get it to a meaty consistency by gradually adding in tablespoons of flour and mixing with my hands. When it finally holds together, I'll shape it into 4–6 balls, and then set them aside.

In the meantime, I've let the 12-inch Dutch oven get heated up over a bunch of burning coals, with a bit of oil in the bottom. I'll shape the balls into a patty in my palm and set them into the heated Dutch oven (no lid) to fry. I want it to be really hot so I'll get a good sear. There's nothing in the patty that's not already cooked, so it's not the same as cooking a burger through. Just get a good sear and flip it. It should hold together nicely with the flour binding it.

Then, serve it with ketchup, mustard, and whatever other toppings you have!

TVP MEATLOAF

In addition to being based on shelf-stable ingredients, this one is vegetarian as well. There's a lot of overlap, it seems, between the worlds of vegetarianism and preparation storage, because meat is so hard to keep.

In this recipe, the bulgur wheat gives the meatloaf substance and helps to hold it together. You could easily double this recipe in a 12-inch Dutch oven.

TOOLS

10-inch Dutch oven
16 coals below (for boiling the water)
8 coals below (for baking)
16 coals above (for baking)

INGREDIENTS

1 cup textured vegetable protein (TVP)
1 cup bulgur wheat
1 cup oatmeal
1¼ cups water

½ cup dehydrated bell pepper
½ cup dehydrated onion
1 (1/16 ounce) pkg. dry onion soup mix
salt
pepper
garlic powder
herbs or spices, of your choice

¾ cup ketchup

AFTER THE coals are lit and getting white, I put them under the Dutch oven and add the water. Then, I'll cover the Dutch oven and let the water boil. The low quantity means that it won't take long. Once it boils, I'll pull it off the coals and add in the first set of ingredients. After stirring, I let it soak up the hot water for 15 to 20 minutes.

Then, I add in all of the flavorings, stirring and letting that soak. I'll shape the mixture into the Dutch oven. If it's a bit dry, you can add water, and if it's too wet, add more bulgur or oatmeal. Don't add too much of either one. Just a tiny bit at a time to make adjustments.

Once it's formed in the bottom of the Dutch oven and made to the right consistency, I'll spread the ketchup over the top and set it up on the coals as outlined above. Then, I let it bake for 1 hour to 1 hour and 15 minutes. When it's done, I'll let it cool a bit and serve!

PEARLED BARLEY AND GROUND BEEF SOUP

Barley and beef is a staple from my own memories. Of course, even though my mom used to make it, most of the time it came out of a can. Canned soups will store nicely on the shelf, but you can't beat the flexibility of storing ingredients and making the dishes yourself.

Pearl barley is the best kind of barley for soups. It's essentially barley with the hull and the bran removed. This makes it cook much more quickly and easily.

TOOLS
12-inch Dutch oven
22+ coals underneath

8-inch Dutch oven
10+ coals underneath

INGREDIENTS
8–10 cups water
1 cup pearled barley

2 cups freeze-dried ground beef or beef TVP
½ cup freeze-dried chopped onion (I really like onions so I put in 1 cup)
½ cup freeze-dried carrots
½ cup freeze-dried celery
1 Tbsp. freeze-dried minced garlic or garlic powder

1 (6-oz.) can tomato paste
4 Tbsp. beef bouillon
salt
pepper
2 crumbled bay leaves
parsley
optional shakes of chili powder, cumin, or cinnamon

THE FIRST thing to do is to get some coals hot and start boiling water. I'll put a second, smaller pot (in this case, the 8-inch) on coals with water to boil as well. That way, later in the cooking process, if I need to add water, it will already be hot. I also make sure to cover the Dutch ovens to help the water boil.

Once the water in the 12-inch Dutch oven is boiling, I add in the barley and let it cook for a while, maybe a half hour or so. It won't be fully cooked at that point, but it will have a good start. Then, I'll add in the dehydrated ingredients. I'll let it simmer more, and then I'll judge the level of the liquid in the soup. If you like it brothy and thin, add more hot water. If you like it more hearty and chunky, add less water.

Finally, at that point, I'll add in the flavorings that I want. I'll taste it and add what's missing to my palate. Then I'll let it simmer for a while to blend and taste again.

EASY BEEF STROGANOFF

I LOVE beef stroganoff. I've tasted many different variations of it. My favorite is a little unorthodox: I like it with feta cheese sprinkled on top for serving. Unfortunately, I've not found a decent shelf-stable feta. Maybe you could use a hard, grated cheese, like Parmesan.

TOOLS

10-inch Dutch oven
15+ coals below (for the noodles)
8 coals below (for the baking)
12 coals above (for the baking)

INGREDIENTS

4 cups water
1 (16-oz.) pkg. egg noodles

2½ cups freeze-dried ground beef or beef TVP
½ cup freeze-dried chopped onion
1 (10.5-oz.) can cream of mushroom soup
½ tsp. paprika
½ cup dehydrated sour cream

ONCE THE coals are getting white, I'll start this one by heating the water in a covered Dutch oven until it's boiling. Then, I'll add in the noodles. I'll let them cook until it's boiling again, maybe another 5–10 minutes. Since the noodles will continue to cook with the other ingredients, they don't have to be completely done in the water. Once they're almost "al dente," I'll pull them out with a spaghetti spoon and set them aside in a bowl.

Then, in the remaining heated water, I'll add in the dehydrated beef and onion and let them absorb the liquid. Finally, I'll add the soup, the paprika, and the sour cream. I'll also add in any other seasonings (salt, pepper, maybe parsley) that I want.

Finally, I'll stir the noodles back in and set the coals as shown above. I'll bake it to heat it through for another 15–20 minutes or so. Then, it's ready to serve!

OLD TIME BEEF STEW

This is a food-storage, shelf-stable take on an old comfort-food dish!

TOOLS
12-inch Dutch oven
20+ coals below

INGREDIENTS
5 cups water
2 cups freeze-dried roast beef
½ cup dehydrated carrots
½ cup freeze-dried tomato chunks
½ cup freeze-dried green pepper
½ cup freeze-dried celery
½ cup dehydrated onion

2 Tbsp. vegetable oil
2 cups water
1 Tbsp. Worcestershire sauce
1 Tbsp. garlic powder
1–2 bay leaves
1 tsp. salt
1 tsp. sugar
½ tsp. pepper
½ tsp. paprika

1 Tbsp. cornstarch

THE PROCESS for this recipe is a little different because we want to brown the meat a little and get some caramelization for richer flavor. That means we'll want to reconstitute everything before we mix the stew.

I'll start with the Dutch oven on the coals with 5 cups water and a lid on. I'll have the dehydrated meat and veggies in different bowls, waiting. Once the water is boiling, I'll add 2 cups of the water to the bowl with the meat and the rest of the water into the bowl with the veggies. I'll let them sit for a while and reconstitute.

I'll put the Dutch oven back on the coals (which might need to be replenished) and let it dry. Then, I'll put the oil in the bottom and let it heat up. Once it's shimmery, I'll get the meat ready by draining it and tossing it into the Dutch oven. It'll sizzle and brown. I'm wanting to get that grilled look.

Then, I'll add in the veggies, 2 cups water, and the rest of the flavorings. I'll close it up and let it simmer for a long time to develop the flavors. After about an hour, I'll draw out a cup of the liquid (without ingredients), put it in another bowl, and whisk in the cornstarch. Once it's nicely dissolved, I'll add it back into the simmering broth. This will thicken it into almost a sauce and make it more of a stew than a soup.

I suggest serving this with biscuits.

BEEF AND BISCUITS

TOOLS
12-inch Dutch Oven
10–12 coals below
16–18 coals above

INGREDIENTS
2 (12-oz.) cans roast beef (usually with gravy)
½ cup dehydrated onion
½ cup dehydrated green peppers
2–3 (14.5-oz.) cans various vegetables (corn, beans, peas, and so on, including liquid)
1 (4-oz.) can mushrooms (including liquid)
1 cube beef bouillon

water (if needed)
1–2 Tbsp. cornstarch (if needed to thicken stew)

1 recipe biscuits (use the basic master mix and biscuit recipe in the breads section, pages 71–72)

WE START, as always, by lighting up some coals. While that's getting white-edged and ready, I'll mix everything in the first set into the

Dutch oven. Then, I'll set that on the coals with the lid on (and coals on the lid). I'll let that start to simmer. After it's simmered a little, I'll check the consistency. If it's too thin, stir some cornstarch into a little bit of hot water, and add it to the broth. If it's too thick, or there's no gravy, add some water, and possibly some cornstarch for texture.

While it's heating and simmering, I'll mix the biscuit dough. You can use either the recipe for drop biscuits or disc biscuits (pages 72–73). The drop ones are a little easier to work with, but the disc ones are flakier. Do what you like!

Make sure there are plenty of fresh coals on the lid. You'll want that to be as hot as possible. Once the biscuits are mixed and prepared, I'll return to the stew and layer biscuit discs or drop the dough balls onto the bubbling stew. I'll close up the heated lid, and let it bake for 15–20 minutes more.

The beef stew steams the biscuits and infuses the flavor into them. It all turns out rich and hearty!

HOT AND SOUR SOUP

This is a delicious Asian-inspired soup that's quite hearty but also works well as a side dish. I suggest serving it with some rice on the side if it is the main dish.

If you have some fresh eggs, you can make this as egg-drop soup, but I wouldn't recommend reconstituted eggs for this. It's still yummy without them.

TOOLS

10-inch or 12-inch Dutch oven

15–18 coals underneath for the 10-inch
20+ coals underneath for the 12-inch

INGREDIENTS

4 cups chicken broth
2 cups water
1 (8- to 10-oz.) bag of dried tofu cubes
½ cup dehydrated onions
½ cup dehydrated celery

2 (12.5-oz.) cans chicken breast
2 (5-oz.) cans bamboo shoots, shredded
5 Tbsp. rice vinegar (or any type of vinegar)
2 Tbsp soy sauce
½–1 tsp. white pepper
3 tsp. sesame oil
1 tsp. powdered ginger

¼ cup water, as needed
2 Tbsp. cornstarch, as needed

optional ingredients:
dried Thai chiles
2 eggs (do not substitute; leave out if you don't have eggs)

AFTER HEATING up the coals, I get this dish going by heating up the broth and water. This is an estimated amount, by the way. The actual amount of liquid you use is determined by how much is absorbed by the dehydrated ingredients and how runny you like your soup. Once it's hot and even starting to boil, I'll add in the dehydrated ingredients and let them start to simmer and reconstitute. Liquids boil better when the Dutch oven lid is on, by the way.

Once they're looking plump and the broth is starting to simmer, I'll add in the ingredients and flavorings in the second set. If you have them and you like spicy foods, add a few dried Thai chiles. Adjust all of the flavorings to taste. If you don't have white pepper, use black. The soy sauce will give you the salty taste.

Once it's simmering lightly, I'll add the eggs. This is kinda tricky, and you can do it how you like. I'll crack the eggs into a separate bowl, and break them up with a fork. I don't say *beat* them, because I don't want them whipped into a yellow liquid, but rather I want it to still have some distinction between the egg white and the yolk, but still have them stirred together somewhat.

Then, I'll drizzle that around into the soup. Don't stir it right away. Give it 2–3 minutes in the hot simmering broth first. That will cook the threads of egg into nice big strands. If you stir it right away, it will break up the egg into tiny particles. After 2–3 minutes, you should see the egg flowing in the convection of the broth, and then you can gently stir.

At that point, adjust the consistency of the soup. If it's too chunky, add more hot water. If it's too runny, mix some cornstarch into hot water and pour it by the tablespoon into the soup, stirring. That will smooth and thicken it into a silky consistency. Not quite a gravy, but not a soup, either.

You can also add noodles, dried shiitake mushrooms, or any other veggies you like. As I said before, I'd serve it with a nice steaming ball of rice!

TACO SOUP MIX

This is kind of a cool home-storage trick. You can make up this mix and store it in quart jars, and then when you want the soup, just add it to the Dutch oven with the water. You can multiply it out to make many jars, but in order to keep the proportions right, measure each ingredient into each jar.

TOOLS

12-inch Dutch oven
20+ coals below

INGREDIENTS

6–8 cups water or chicken broth

2 cups quick cook red beans
1 cup taco TVP
½ cup dehydrated sliced onion
⅓ cup freeze-dried bell peppers
¾ cup freeze-dried corn
½ cup tomato powder
1 (1-oz.) pkg. taco seasoning

GATHER UP all of the ingredients and add them one at a time into a quart jar. The beans are instant, precooked beans so it doesn't have to simmer for a week to get soft. Add an oxygen packet on top and seal up the jar to store.

Then, some time later, it's time to cook!

First, I'll get some hot coals under the Dutch oven, and add in the water or broth. It can be all water, all broth, or a mix of the two. I'll put the lid on and let it boil.

Once it's boiling, I'll add in the other ingredients. Then it just has to simmer long enough for the beans to be cooked, for the veggies and the TVP to reconstitute, and for the flavors to blend. About a half hour should do it!

CHAPTER 2

BREADS

BREADS ARE at the core of just about all human diets, even though their popularity goes up and down from year to year. If you're wanting to store food and bake loaves of bread, you have to be aware of some things that make it a little difficult. A number of ingredients don't have the long-lasting shelf life of ingredients like beans or TVP.

One issue is the flour itself. The best way to store flour is as wheat berries, to be ground and used almost immediately. Wheat has natural oils in it, which, when exposed to oxygen, can go rancid. In consequence, if the wheat is stored dried, airtight, and unground, it can store for many years. However, if you grind it into flour, then the oils are exposed to air, causing the oils to go rancid after some time.

Another issue is that grinding wheat is great for whole wheat recipes (there are some below), but what of recipes that use regular white flour or bread flour? All-purpose flour can store for as long as 8 months, cool and dry, but it will eventually go bad. Bread flour can get old in as little as a month. In that case, not only will it go rancid but it will also not produce gluten as easily. Isn't that the whole reason to use bread flour?

Many bread, roll, and biscuit recipes require adding even more oils, such as butter, shortening, or vegetable oil. These can be stored in the short run, and it's also possible to use versions of these that are powdered and canned. The same issue comes up with eggs, milk, and other enrichments.

With chemical leavens (like baking powder or baking soda), there is little concern for shelf life, as they are both quite stable. Even still, over extended periods of time, the acid and base in a baking powder can combine with water vapor in the air, causing the powder to lose potency.

Yeast is another matter altogether. In a factory sealed container, yeast can store for as long as two years. Once it's been opened, however, its fresh life expectancy is only a few months or up to four months in the fridge. Buying the small packets might be more expensive per unit, but you're only exposing as much as you're using each time.

With that understanding, you can use these recipes with the ingredients that you have in short-term, medium-term, or long-term storage.

We're going to start with some quick breads, using chemical leavens. This is where a chemical reaction between an acid and a base in your bread will create bubbles of carbon dioxide in the dough. When these hit the heat of the Dutch oven, they expand and then set as the heat fixes the crumb structure in place.

The Basic Master Mix

First, though, we have to make the basic mix. So often when we want to make biscuits to go along with a meal, we simply reach for the box of biscuit mix. We add in the water, and away we go. Remember, the chemicals won't begin reacting until moisture is added. The cool thing about the box is that this mix isn't just for biscuits. With the right additives and enrichments, you can make pancakes, muffins, waffles, dumplings, and many other bread-y stuff. Just reach for the box.

Well, here, we like to work from scratch, but we still like the convenience. So, start off by making up your own mix. Then, when you need it, it's there. This makes the whole experience that much quicker. It contains shortening, or oils, so the mix itself is not good for long-term storage. The ingredients, however, last longer, so you can store them and make more mix as you need it!

BASIC MASTER MIX

INGREDIENTS

20 cups flour
2½ cups powdered milk (unmixed—still a powder)
¾ cup double acting baking powder
3 Tbsp. salt
2 Tbsp. cream of tartar
½ cup sugar

1 lb. vegetable shortening or reconstituted shortening powder

FIRST, SIFT or whisk all of the first set of ingredients together. Mix it well, as the entire quantity needs to be an even balance of all of the ingredients.

Then, use a pastry cutter to cut in the shortening until it looks well blended, like cornmeal. You can even use your hands to work out some of the bigger chunks.

Once it's all mixed, store it in larger zip-top bags or another airtight container in a cool, dry place. It keeps well for 6–8 weeks. You can use it in your recipes. Another way to keep it longer is to mix larger quantities with everything but the fats and make smaller batches from that (oil added) for more frequent, temporary use. You can store the smaller quantities in the zip-top bags.

Here are a couple of ways to use this mix to make quick bread biscuits.

DROP BISCUITS

I like to do drop biscuits because they're much easier than rolled biscuits. You just mix it up and spoon it into the Dutch oven to cook. It's ready.

TOOLS
12-inch Dutch oven
12–15 coals below
24–28 coals above

INGREDIENTS
3 cups basic master mix
¾–1 cup water or milk, cold, if possible (It could be reconstituted instant fat-free milk. Remember that there is milk powder in the basic mix too.)

START BY lighting up the coals and letting them get white. Then, spritz or smear the Dutch oven interior with some oil and set it on and under the coals. You'll notice that there are a LOT of coals. The Dutch oven needs to be very hot to activate the chemical reaction and to swell the gas bubbles.

Then stir up the mix and the water. You want it to be a bit sticky and gooey. Flour absorbs water differently in different circumstances, so simply add enough water to make it look sticky. It's not a batter, but it's not a tight, smooth ball of dough, either. Stir it up, but don't work it. It won't be kneaded.

Open up the Dutch oven and drop generous spoonfuls into it. Arrange them in the bottom and close the lid as quickly as you can so that it loses as little heat as possible. Check them in 10–15 minutes. The biscuits should be fluffy and only slightly browned.

Pull them out using a spatula and arrange them on cooling racks. It's important to let breads cool because much of the process of cooking is still happening. You can mix up more dough and bake more biscuits while the first batch is cooling.

GARLIC AND CHEDDAR DROP BISCUITS

Here's a great variation. Add the following ingredients into the mix and follow the exact same procedure as the previous recipe.

INGREDIENTS

3 cups basic master mix
¾–1 cup water or milk, cold, if possible
1 cup shredded cheddar cheese (could be frozen, freeze dried, or dried powder)
1 tsp. garlic powder
2 Tbsp. butter, melted

THESE ARE made in the same way as the previous recipe. Oil and preheat the Dutch oven, and mix the ingredients the same way. Drop the balls of dough into the Dutch oven and bake them for 10–15 minutes; then cool them. These taste especially good with chowders, soups, and seafood dishes.

DISC BISCUITS

NO MATTER what kind of biscuits I'm making, I'll usually follow a similar process. Start by lighting up the coals. Let them start to get a bit white while you gather up the ingredients and prepare your space.

Then, when the coals are white, put the Dutch oven (with some oil spritzed in it) on and under the burning coals to preheat while you mix and prepare the dough. If you're making a big batch, you might even heat up two Dutch ovens.

Start off by measuring out the master mix into a bowl, then adding the liquid. You'll want this to be a drier dough compared to the drop biscuit dough. It should come together in a ball. You might use your hand for some of the mixing, with kind of a kneading motion, but not too much. You don't want to develop any gluten, and you don't want the fats in the mix to get warm and soft. The fats need to stay cool to trap the gas the chemical reaction is making.

Then, dump the dough out on a floured counter and flatten it out (either with a rolling pin or your hands). Flatten it to a ½ or ¾ of an inch. Sprinkle it with some flour, fold it over, and flatten it out again. Repeat this process 4–5 times, creating layers. But don't do this too much. The chemical reaction has been already taking place and you want to get it into the oven as soon as possible.

Then, cut the dough into circles. I'm told that if you use a cup, don't twist it because it can let too much gas out. I've never noticed it that much. After punching out a few circles, wad the remaining dough back up, flatten it again, and cut some more.

At various times, I've coated the tops with milk, butter, or beaten egg. They will give different textures and browning. That's not necessary, though.

Then take the biscuit rounds out and put them in the ovens, which should be pretty hot by now. Close up the lid and mark the time. Check them in about 10 minutes, at which point they'll be done or close to being done. Pull the biscuits out of the Dutch ovens and put them onto cooling racks. Then enjoy them with butter, jam, or honey!

SURVIVAL BARS

When I first saw this recipe, I was very intrigued. The article claimed that it would keep after baking indefinitely. It was called a "survival bread." I mixed it up and baked it, and what I got was a solid brick, tough and dry. The surprise was that my sons gobbled it up and have asked me to make it several times since then. I agree with them that it really tastes great and it's filling too.

I found, however, that presentation and perceptions are important. If you showed it to me as a big round ball doorstop and called it a bread loaf, I probably wouldn't even try it. On the other hand, if it were flat, cut into bars, and slipped into snack-sized baggies, I'd think it was a variant of a granola bar, and I'd eat it without even thinking twice. Funny, huh?

And, since my sons have never let it last longer than a few days, I have no idea what its shelf-life really is.

TOOLS
8-inch Dutch oven
10–14 coals below

12-inch Dutch oven
18–20 coals above
10–12 coals below

INGREDIENTS
about ½ cup water
3 Tbsp. honey
1 (3-oz.) pkg. lemon or orange gelatin

2 cups oats
2½ cups milk powder
1 cup sugar

ONCE THE coals are lit, place about a dozen or so underneath the 8-inch Dutch oven with the water, covered. Let it boil and add the honey and gelatin packet.

While the water is boiling, mix the dry ingredients in a bowl. Let the liquids cool a bit, and then add them to the bowl and stir it all together. It should come together in a big sticky mess, but still hold together like biscuit dough. If it's still too dry, you can add water, a bit at a time.

Oil the bottom and sides of the inside of the 12-inch Dutch oven. Spread the dough evenly around the bottom. Put it on the coals, as listed above, with the lid on, and bake for 35–40 minutes. Turn the Dutch oven and the lid every 10–15 minutes so as to prevent hot spots and burning. After about 25 minutes, check the progress. When it's done, it should be nicely browned on top.

Let it cool and lift it out of the Dutch oven. Cut it into bars, about 1 inch by 3 inch or so.

They're good for on-the-go munching with a bit of water or milk to drink with it.

CRACKERS

Crackers are another great way to carry goodness on the go. Once you've got a good core recipe, you can do quite a bit with it and give it lots of variety. I found this to be a good recipe, although, honestly, they weren't quite as light and fluffy as the ones from the store. The core recipe was delicious, however, and some of our family's flavor variations were yummy too!

To make a good quantity, I'd recommend heating up two Dutch ovens and doubling the recipe. Then, at your prep station, roll out some dough and cut it into shapes. Bake them in batches, and while they're baking, roll out and cut more. I'll describe it in more detail below.

TOOLS

2 (12-inch) shallow Dutch ovens
10–12 coals below
18–20 coals above

INGREDIENTS

2 cups some kind of flour (it can be all-purpose, whole wheat, cornmeal, or a blend)
1 tsp. baking powder
⅓ cup some kind of oil (veggie oil, shortening, butter, and so on)
½ tsp. salt

any flavorings you want to add

about ¾ cup cold water

START BY lighting the coals and, once burning, setting the Dutch ovens on the heat. Oil the insides and let them preheat.

Mix the first set of ingredients. If you're using a solid oil, like shortening or butter, cut it in with a knife or blend it with your hands until it looks like meal. Add in your flavorings. I've done things like garlic powder, cracked pepper, dried herbs, and things like that. You could add cheese powder or even something wet like tomato paste. Whatever you add, put it in by the spoonful and watch to see how it mixes with the whole. Some flavorings, like cheese powder, will require a lot more than, say, pepper or garlic.

Then, mix in the water. Start with a bit less, and add a few drizzles at a time as you mix. The flavorings you've added could easily change the amount of water you need. You want it to come together as a dough ball and not be too sticky.

Roll the dough out between waxed papers to a fine thinness, say, ⅛ inch. Cut them into shapes. I just use a knife and make triangles, but you can do squares and circles. Typically, when you're baking these in your indoor oven, you could just put the rolled out dough on a cookie sheet and cut. It's tough to do the same thing in a Dutch oven, especially one that's been preheated.

Lift the lid on a Dutch oven and lay the crackers in quickly. It's okay if some touch or overlap a little. You can brush or spritz them with a little extra water and sprinkle with more flavorings, like kosher salt. Put the heated lid back on and mark the time. Then cut some more and put them into the other Dutch oven. Go back to the prep table and roll out some more dough. After 10–15 minutes, check on the first Dutch oven. It should be just a bit browned. Lift them out with a spatula and put in another batch.

Let them cool, as they'll get crisper as they do. Serve them with a good soup or chili, or pack them into plastic zip-tops for later munching!

Here are some fun flavor combinations:

½ cup cheddar powder

1 tsp. garlic powder

2–4 Tbsp. tomato paste
1 tsp. garlic powder

shakes of dried oregano and basil

1 Tbsp. lemon juice or lime juice
Brush the top with extra juice and sprinkle kosher salt

2–3 Tbsp. of a mix packet (ranch dip, taco seasoning, or a French onion soup)

CORNY CORN BREAD

Corn bread is a big favorite of mine. It's a delicious side with a good, hearty chili or stew and can be served with roasts or just about any other kind of main dish. It's very traditional. There are lots of different base recipes for corn bread. This one is nice in that it actually includes corn, not just cornmeal, for extra texture and sweetness. This one has two ways of baking (see below).

TOOLS
10-inch Dutch oven
8 coals below
16 coals above

INGREDIENTS
1 cup cornmeal
1 cup all-purpose flour
3 tsp. baking powder
½ tsp. salt
¼ cup dry milk
¼ cup sugar
2 tsp. powdered egg whites

1 (14.5-oz.) can creamed corn
½ cup water
2 Tbsp. oil

BEGIN BY lighting and heating up the coals. As they're getting white edges, mix all of the dry ingredients in a bowl. Whisk those together to blend them well. Then, add in the wet ingredients in the second set, and whisk until it's well blended.

Set the Dutch oven on the coals and spread or spray a bit of oil in the interior. Put on the lid and put the coals on top. Let that preheat for 12–15 minutes. Then pour the mix in and close up the lid. After about 15 minutes, rotate the lid and the Dutch oven each a quarter turn to prevent hot spots and burning. After another 15 minutes or so, check on the bread. Dip a toothpick in and see if it comes out clean. Is the top browned a bit? If so, it's done.

This can also be done with just bottom heat, either with coals or by suspending the Dutch oven over a campfire. You'd want 16–20 coals below or a pretty hot bed of campfire coals. If you're using a campfire, don't put the Dutch oven directly onto the coals, but use a tripod to suspend it above. In either case, the bread will "poof" more if the oven is preheated.

FOOD STORAGE PIZZA

Making a fresh pizza with dough that's risen overnight and topping it with fresh cheeses, veggies, and meats creates a pizza with incredible flavor. It's also, unfortunately, the exact opposite of "shelf stable." The bread flour you'd want to use would get stale in just a month, and the meats, veggies, and cheeses would go bad very quickly.

Because of this, we make substitutions so that if you're in a bind and working with your shelf-stable food storage, you can still have tasty pizza. Maybe it won't taste quite like pizza made with fully fresh ingredients, but it will still taste great. If you have some fresh ingredients, by all means, use them.

TOOLS
12-inch shallow Dutch oven
10–12 coals below
18–22 coals above

8-inch Dutch oven
15 coals underneath

THE CRUST
1 box pre-purchased pizza dough mix. Alternately, make a batch of biscuit dough from the Basic Master Mix listed at the start of this chapter (page 71).

THE SAUCE
1 (6-oz.) can tomato sauce or reconstituted tomato powder, mixed to the desired consistency.
Liberal shakes of garlic powder, oregano, basil, salt, and pepper. I like to add a little cayenne.

THE TOPPINGS
1 (6–8-oz.) can mushrooms (sliced or cut into pieces)
reconstituted TVP meats, especially sausage, beef, and bacon flavors
canned meats (chicken, ham, sausage, shrimp, anchovies)
reconstituted freeze dried cheeses, especially mozzarella
reconstituted dried veggies (peppers, onions, sun-dried tomatoes)
anything else you can imagine

START THE coals, and when they're getting hot, put some under the 8-inch Dutch oven (covered) with some water. As that heats or boils, use it to reconstitute any dried or freeze-dried toppings. Usually, that means mixing the dried food in a bowl with hot water. Follow the instructions that come with your brand of dried foods.

Also, spread some coals on the lid of the 12-inch Dutch oven so it can start to preheat.

Mix the crust. It won't be the same as a traditional pizza crust, but it will still taste good. Also, mix the sauce ingredients. Oil the bottom of the 12-inch Dutch oven, kinda liberally. I like to sprinkle some seasonings on the bottom as well, like some garlic powder, salt, and paprika. That will season the bottom of your crust.

Then, spread the dough out over the bottom of the Dutch oven. Spoon on some sauce and spread it to the edges of the pizza. Sprinkle on a little cheese and begin to scatter on the topping ingredients you choose. I like to have lots of toppings on my pizzas. Some like theirs to be sparse. You do as you like. Finally, smother it all under another layer of cheese and set the Dutch oven on the coals. Add the heated lid and adjust the coals, top and bottom, to the proper amount.

After about 15 minutes, turn the lid and the Dutch oven so as to prevent hot spots and burning. Check to see how it is, quickly. It's likely that it will need another 10–15 minutes. When the cheese is all melted (maybe even a little browned) and the crust is puffed up, it's done. Let it cool a little, and then slice it and serve it straight from the Dutch oven!

PEANUT BUTTER BREAD

TOOLS
10-inch Dutch oven
6–8 coals below
12–14 coals above

INGREDIENTS
2½ cup flour
3 tsp. baking powder

½ tsp. salt
⅔ cup sugar
⅓ cup instant nonfat dry milk powder

½ cup peanut butter (or ¼ cup peanut butter powder and ¼ cup water)

1 egg beaten (or 2 Tbsp. whole egg powder + 3 Tbsp. water)
¾ cup water

1 Tbsp. dried orange rind (or 1 tsp. orange flavoring) (optional)

START UP some coals and, while they're getting white and hot, start to mix the ingredients.

Start with the dry ingredients. Mix them in a bowl, whisking to get them all stirred and blended together. Add in the peanut butter and cut it into the powders. This can be done with a pastry blender or by just using a couple of butter knives.

Once that's well blended, add the egg (reconstituted if it was dry) and the water. Add in the orange rind and mix it well.

Grease the interior of a Dutch oven with spray oil or shortening and spread the batter over the bottom. Set the Dutch oven onto a ring of coals with coals on the lid (as described above) and let it bake. Every 15 minutes, rotate the Dutch oven and the lid each a quarter turn to prevent hot spots and burning. In 45 minutes to an hour, it should be baked and a toothpick should come out clean.

HONDURAN BALEADAS: FLOUR TORTILLAS AND REFRIED BEANS

A lot of years ago (I won't say how many or I'd give away my advanced age), I spent a few years working for my church in Honduras. Even though I wasn't that much into cooking way back then, I enjoyed experiencing their culture through their food while I was living there. Honduran cuisine is rich and diverse, but in many cases it's driven by deep poverty. Simple ingredients combined in creative ways and cooked in primitive kitchens often define the flavors.

I found this recipe online, and not only is it delicious and shelf-stable, but it also reminded me of dinners in Honduras.

Honduran tortillas, most often, are handmade corn tortillas, unlike the machine-made ones that I found during my time in Belize. When they do use flour tortillas, they're puffier than the thin, flat tortillas we often find in southwestern/Mexican restaurants here in America.

In Honduras, they cook the flour tortillas very much like they do the corn tortillas—on a flat metal skillet or sheet over a fire or hot plate. For our experience, we'll cook them on the lid of a Dutch oven, inverted over some coals.

TOOLS

12-inch Dutch oven lid, with a trivet
24+ coals below

12-inch Dutch oven
20–24 coals below

INGREDIENTS

4–5 cups flour
1½ tsp. baking powder
1½ tsp. salt
1 egg (can be reconstituted from powder)
⅓ cup oil or shortening
about 1 cup cold water

2–3 cups of cooked beans (kidney, pinto, black, or any other type—they could even be mixed)
topping ingredients

IF THE beans are still hard—dried beans, uncooked—you'll want to start by preparing those first. If they're canned or you've already cooked them (maybe they're leftovers), then you can skip ahead.

When I do beans for a soup, stew, chili, or other dish, I'll start with the beans by soaking them the overnight, or at least 4–6 hours. Beans are very hard and don't take on water easily. They will cook very slowly if you haven't pre-soaked them. Make sure that you put in enough water to cover the beans and add a few extra inches. As they soak, they'll take up most, if not all, of the water.

By the way, I'm told that mixing different beans together will form more complete proteins, which is better for you.

When they've soaked and the time comes to cook, drain off any water in the soaking bowl and dump them into your Dutch oven. Put in enough water to cover the beans and put the Dutch oven on 20–24 coals. Cover it up. The heavy lid will trap most of the hot steam and will help it boil and cook faster. Bring it up to a boil and then set the coals to a steady simmer. Even though this method is "faster," it's still not "fast." It will take 2–3 hours to cook the beans. Keep the lid on most of the time, except to stir and check on it. You'll want to keep a side fire of coals going to replenish the heat. Every 20 minutes or so, put another 6–8 coals in your chimney or on your fire, and then add a few more under the Dutch oven.

Once the beans are soft and done (not al dente, but soft), take them off the fire and drain them. Set them aside. We'll come back to the beans in a bit.

If your beans are already canned or if they're about done in the pot, you can focus on the tortillas. Start by whisking the flour, the baking powder, and the salt in a bowl to blend them well. If you're using shortening or some other solid fat, cut that into the meal mix next. Use a pastry cutter or a pair of butter knives to mix it all together nicely. If not, add liquid oil with the other wet ingredients.

Make a well in the middle of the powder and add the egg (fresh or reconstituted from powder), the oil (if not using shortening), and some of the water. Begin mixing the dough with your hands, adding small amounts of water, until it pulls away from the bowl.

Pull the dough out of the bowl and begin kneading in earnest on the tabletop, continuing for 8–10 minutes. If the dough is still dry, you can add more water by drizzling some on your hands as you knead. Oil can also be used on your hands to keep the dough from sticking so much.

The kneading process will activate the flour's natural gluten and will help the dough become a bit elastic. When you're finished, shape the dough into balls about the size of something between a golf ball and a tennis ball. Pull the dough back and stretch it around on itself.

Press the bottom into a seam, so that the upper surface stretches a little. Set these balls aside to rest for 20 minutes or so.

While the dough balls are resting, you can work on the beans and get the Dutch ovens ready.

Using the remaining coals from cooking the beans, heat up some fresh coals. Do a lot, like 40 or more. Shake or stir them occasionally to make sure they're more evenly lit. Once they're white-edged, put half under your 12-inch Dutch oven and put the rest around a metal trivet or lid stand. Invert the Dutch oven lid on the trivet over the coals so that it becomes a griddle. Let them both heat up. Heat a few tablespoons of oil or shortening in the bottom of the Dutch oven.

Take the beans and mash them with a potato masher or a slotted spoon. How coarsely or finely you mash them will be up to your taste. If you have electricity, you could run them through a blender. Then, pour the mashed beans into the Dutch oven. Work the beans so the oil begins to incorporate into them. The beans should start to fry in your "pan."

The griddle (lid) temperature is very important. It should be very uncomfortable to hold your hand an inch or so above the griddle. Lightly oil the griddle. Now you're ready!

There are lots of methods to flatten the tortillas. One is to press them between two sturdy plastic or metal plates (using waxed paper to keep them loose). Another is to use a commercially available tortilla press. This usually has two metal or wooden plates and a handle to press one of the plates onto the other. A third method is to simply roll them out with a rolling pin.

Drop a flattened tortilla onto the griddle and let it cook until brown spots appear on the bottom, then flip it for the other side. It should poof up some. When it's done, spread some bean mash onto one side, add any cheeses or other toppings you might have, and double it over. Serve it right away or cook a batch of tortillas and assemble and serve them afterward.

FRIED BREAD

Here's a variant of the previous recipe that I came across. This one doesn't use an egg, nor does it use as much kneading or resting. That's not going to be critical. Also, we'll be frying the bread. Deep-frying is difficult in a Dutch oven, as it's hard to heat the oil hot enough and to maintain that temperature. I prefer to "shallow" fry in a smaller Dutch oven so that it doesn't require as much oil and heat.

TOOLS
10-inch Dutch oven
15–18 coals underneath (really, as much as you can pack under it)

INGREDIENTS
oil for frying
2¼ cups flour
1 tsp. baking powder
½ tsp. salt
1 Tbsp. shortening
¾ cup water

IF YOU want to serve this with beans, just follow the same process as the previous recipe.

Light up some coals. When they're getting a bit white, put them under your Dutch oven, with up to a half inch of oil in the bottom. Let that heat up.

Start the bread by mixing the flour, baking powder, and salt in a bowl. Add in the shortening, and cut it in with a pastry cutter, a couple of knives, or just blend with your hand. Add the water and continue mixing. If you need to add more water or flour, do so in small quantities as you're mixing.

Pinch off pieces that are about the size of a golf ball, or even a little bigger. Flatten it in the palm of your hand (you can use flour or oil to keep it from sticking), and lay it into the pot of oil. Fry it until it's brown, then turn it over.

When it's done, let it drain on a paper towel and serve it. It can be eaten as is, as a side, with beans, or sprinkled with cinnamon sugar as a dessert or treat.

EZEKIEL BREAD

This bread takes its name from the Bible, from Ezekiel 4:9, which says, "Take thou also unto thee wheat, and barley, and beans, and lentils, and millet, and fitches, and put them in one vessel, and make thee bread thereof, according to the number of the days that thou shalt lie upon thy side, three hundred and ninety days shalt thou eat thereof."

The idea is that this bread is supposedly nutritionally complete, as Ezekiel lived off it in his day. It's actually quite delicious, and, as food storage, excellent in that it's ground and made on the fly rather than by trying to keep flour over time.

TOOLS
12-inch Dutch oven
10–12 coals below
16–20 coals above

INGREDIENTS
2½ cups wheat berries
1½ cups spelt flour
½ cup barley
½ cup millet
¼ cup dry green lentils
2 Tbsp. dry great northern beans
2 Tbsp. dry kidney beans
2 Tbsp. dried pinto beans (or about a half cup of any combination you have of dried beans)
3 cups hot tap water

1 cup hot tap water
1 cup honey
2 Tbsp. active dry yeast

½ cup olive oil
2 teaspoons salt

START BY mixing all of the grains and beans together in a bowl. Blend them together as well as you can, then add them to a grinder (powered or hand-driven) and grind them as fine as you can. Add the hot tap water and set it aside for 30–45 minutes to soak. This will allow the ground wheat to develop some gluten and will help it rise.

Then, while the mix is soaking, mix a cup of hot water and a cup of honey together. When it's all blended, it should be warm, at about 110 degrees. It can be cooler than that, but not hotter. If it's cooler, the yeast won't activate quite as well, but if it's hotter, especially at 120 degrees, it can kill the yeast completely. Add the yeast to this mixture, stir, and set aside for 10–15 minutes.

With the ground flour soaked and the yeast mix getting frothy, mix them together and add the oil and salt. Stir them all together. Pour that blend into a greased Dutch oven and let it set aside for about an hour or so, perhaps longer. Check on the rise occasionally.

At about 45 minutes into the rise, light some coals. When they're getting white, put about 18–20 coals on the lid of the Dutch oven and let it preheat for a while.

Finally, as the dough rises and the lid becomes heated, put the lid on the Dutch oven and adjust coals to match above configuration. Bake it for 30–45 minutes or until the internal temperature is at 180–200 degrees.

Let it cool and slice it up!

SHELF-STABLE WHOLE WHEAT BREAD

One of the problems with doing breads with long-term storage is that not all of the ingredients are shelf-stable. The flour is a particular culprit. The wheat grain is easy to store, but as soon as it's ground, the inner parts are exposed to the air and begin to degrade. This is especially true of bread flour. I don't like to make bread with flour that's more than a month or two opened. I just don't get as much gluten nor as much rise.

Add to that the problem that whole wheat flour doesn't develop much gluten anyway. That leaves you stuck with a lot of compromise. To get the lift and the fluff that the gluten gives, a lot of people will add fresh bread flour to the whole wheat, usually at a ratio 70 percent whole wheat to 30 percent white bread flour. That works, but the problem, again, is storage.

On the other hand, baking a loaf out of fresh-ground whole wheat flour works very nicely, but it won't have the gluten, so it won't get all stretchy and fluffy. It'll be more dense and crumbly. Still edible, of course, but not what most folks are used to.

This recipe takes a bit longer because the ground flour presoaks. This helps boost the gluten development so that it can trap the gas the yeast makes and rise more fluffy.

TOOLS
12-inch shallow Dutch oven
12–14 coals below
26–28 coals above

INGREDIENTS
3 cups whole wheat flour
3 cups warm water

½ Tbsp. yeast
½ cup water
¼ cup liquid honey
6 Tbsp. butter, melted fresh or mixed from powder
1 egg, fresh or mixed from powder
2 tsp. salt
2–3 cups whole wheat flour, more for kneading

I STARTED this whole experiment out by grinding up some wheat (I use an electric grinder, but you can do an hand-cranker if you really want to). I combined about 3 cups of the flour with an equal amount of water (almost hot works very well to be absorbed). I let that sit for a long time, about an hour or two. The intent is not to have this rise since we haven't added any yeast yet. We just want to coax the gluten strands into forming.

When I came back, it was gooey, stringy, stretchy, and sticky. Yuck. But no matter. I mixed the yeast with the additional hot water (just hot to the touch, no hotter), and let it sit to get foamy and active.

I added the yeast mix and all of the other ingredients into the mixing bowl with the flour mix (add only 1 or 2 of the final cups of whole-wheat flour). It was kinda hard to stir because the gluten had had a lot of time to develop with the liquid. Once all of the ingredients were well incorporated, I turned it out of the bowl and onto my kitchen counter (well-floured with whole wheat flour). I began to knead it, sprinkling on more whole-wheat flour as I went, just enough to keep it not too sticky on my hands. I was really pleased to feel the gluten tugging on it. It was coming together much more so than any other whole wheat loaf I'd done before. Finally, it passed the stretchy windowpane translucence test!

I shaped it into a boule and set it aside in an oiled bowl to rise. I sprayed on a light coating of oil to help it not dry out, and then covered it and let it rise for a couple of hours.

Since the gluten had developed so well, it rose quite fully and quickly. After the first rise, I quickly reshaped the dough into a boule, pinched a seam at the "bottom," and set it aside, seam-side up. I have a couple of cloth-lined baskets that I use for this second rise, called my "proofing baskets." As I was doing this, it was good to see a nice, tight surface. That showed that there was, in fact, good, stretchy gluten!

I lit up the coals and let them get white edges. Once there were enough ready, I oiled the inside of the Dutch oven and set the coals below it and on the lid to preheat it.

Once the Dutch oven was preheated, it was time to bake. I lifted the lid and quickly upturned the proofing basket into the middle of the Dutch oven. Now, the seam side, the "bottom," was back on the bottom, and the stretchy clean surface was on top. This I sliced a couple of times with a sharp knife to help it vent and "bloom" in the initial spring. I quickly covered it back up with the heated lid and marked the time.

After about 15 minutes, I turned the lid about quarter of the way and then lifted the Dutch oven and turned it a quarter turn as well. After about 30 minutes, I checked it, and it was looking nice and brown, but not done yet. I poked it with the thermometer and dropped the lid. After another 10 minutes or so, I looked again and saw that the bread had reached it's done-ness temperature, 180–190°F (being a darker bread).

Then I lifted it out and set it onto a cooling rack. It really tasted great, and I was surprised by the lightness of the texture with traditionally heavy bread like 100 percent whole wheat. It was very fluffy. Not like a French bread, to be sure, but still very palatable. So, I will always do a pre-soak with the non-glutinous flours. It worked wonders!

CHAPTER 3

DESSERTS

YES, EMERGENCY preparedness is all about surviving and being able to overcome emergencies, struggles, and hard times. I get that.

However, as I said in the beginning, we don't want to just survive. It's not a bad thing to be able to enjoy yourself, even in times of difficulty. That's why, in my family's emergency storage, we've included small games, sketch pads, and diversions. That's also why, in this book, I'm including dessert. Because life, no matter how difficult, is more bearable with dessert.

PEACH "SHORTCAKE" WITH STRAWBERRY BASIL SAUCE

This one starts out with drop biscuits from the recipe on page 72. Then the biscuits are smothered in a delicious rehydrated peach syrup and the yummy strawberry basil sauce. It's a wonderful treat, with shelf-stable ingredients. Really, you can use any combination of freeze-dried fruit for this dish. You could do apples instead of peaches, for example, with freeze-dried blueberries or raspberries for the sauce. You could even do two sauces, one dark, one red, for a delicious red, white, and blue final dish!

TOOLS

12-inch Dutch oven (for biscuits)
12–15 coals below
24–28 coals above

12-inch Dutch oven (for the peaches)
20+ coals below

10-inch Dutch oven (for reconstituting and the berry sauce)
16–18 coals below

INGREDIENTS

5–6 cups water
5 cups freeze-dried peach slices (or some other dried fruit)

3 cups Basic Master Mix (page 71)
¾–1 cup water or milk, cold, if possible. It could be reconstituted instant fat-free milk. Remember that there is milk powder in the basic mix too.

3 cups freeze-dried strawberry slices.
1 cup water
basil, to taste

5 tsp. sugar
cinnamon
nutmeg

START BY lighting up enough coals for two Dutch ovens and letting them get white.

Set one 12-inch Dutch oven on more than 20 coals and add 5–6 cups water. Put the lid on and let it heat up. It can boil. Add the peaches or other fruit and let them swell and absorb the water to reconstitute. You'll want to keep an eye on this. If it needs more water, add it, and stir it occasionally to keep it from going dry and burning.

While the fruit is reconstituting, bake the biscuits. Spritz or smear the other 12-inch Dutch oven interior with some oil and set it on and under the coals. You'll notice that there are a LOT of coals. The Dutch oven needs to be very hot to activate the chemical reaction and to swell the gas bubbles.

Then stir up the mix and the water. You want it to be a bit sticky and gooey. Don't knead it. Open up the Dutch oven, and drop generous spoonfuls into it. Arrange them in the bottom and close the lid as quickly as you can, so that it loses as little heat as possible. Check them in about 10–15 minutes. They should be fluffy and only slightly browned.

Pull them out using a spatula and arrange them on cooling racks. You'll also want to put more coals on the side fire to heat up.

Once the biscuits are done, and the peaches well on their way, crush the strawberries into a fine powder in a plastic bag. Put the 8-inch Dutch oven onto the coals and add the berry powder and 1 cup water. Add the water gradually, stirring until you get a sauce-like texture. Add in the basil, to taste. Let that simmer for a while.

Then, turn your attention back to the peaches. They're probably reconstituted by now, or close to it, so drain off any excess water. You'll probably want to refresh the coals under the Dutch oven, so there's plenty of heat. Sprinkle on the sugar and spices and stir it up, sautéing the peaches and creating a caramelized syrup. Don't be afraid to adjust the amount of sugar as necessary.

Assembly is the final step. Serve it up with one or two biscuits on the plate. Pour some of the peaches and syrup over the biscuits, then add on the strawberry sauce over the top. If you have some powdered whipped topping, that would be a perfect finishing touch.

BLUEBERRY ALMOND CAKE

TOOLS

10-inch Dutch oven
8 coals below
12 coals above

INGREDIENTS

2 cups flour
2 tsp. baking powder
¾ tsp. salt

½ cup butter (fresh or reconstituted from powder)
1 cup sugar
1 tsp. vanilla
2 eggs (fresh, or 4 Tbsp. egg powder + 6 Tbsp. water)

½ cup dehydrated fat-free milk
1½ cups freeze-dried blueberries

1 large egg white (fresh and separated, or from a dried whites-only egg powder)
3 Tbsp. sugar
1 cup sliced almonds

START BY lighting up the coals and letting them start to get white and hot. While that's happening, mix your ingredients and prepare your Dutch oven.

Start by mixing the dry first set of ingredients: the flour, baking powder, and salt. Whisk those together and set them aside. Also, mix the milk powder with water to the right consistency.

Then, mix the butter, the cup of sugar, and the vanilla, and cream them all together. If you do this by hand, it can take some time. Without electricity, I use a slotted spoon to mush them together while turning the bowl. I also have a potato masher with circular holes in it, and that works well. Eventually, as you work it, the blend takes on a light and fluffy look. What you're doing is aerating the mix. This will help it to be a lighter, fluffier cake. Add the 2 eggs or egg mixture a bit at a time while you continue blending.

At about this point, the coals should be white-edged and ready. Put the 24 coals on the lid of the Dutch oven and let it preheat. Cut a circle of parchment paper and put it in the bottom of the Dutch oven, lightly sprayed or wiped with oil.

Into the sugar/butter/egg mix, add about a third of the flour, and continue blending. Then, add about a third of the milk, and continue blending. Carry on adding and blending flour and milk until it's all in and well mixed. Then add the blueberries. Pour it onto the parchment in the Dutch oven.

Then crack and separate 1 egg white, or mix one up from powder. Whip it with a whisk or fork a few times, and then add the tablespoons of sugar, and the almonds. Keep stirring until the almonds are well coated and the sugar is dissolved. Finally, pour that mixture over the batter.

Reset the coals to have 8 below and 16 above, and put the lid on. Let it bake for 10–15 minutes and turn the lid about a quarter turn. Also, lift the Dutch oven and rotate it over the coals about a quarter turn. If the coals are burning out, replenish a few, but be cautious to not put too many coals on.

After about a total of 25–35 minutes, check to see if it's done. Use the "toothpick test" to see if an inserted toothpick comes up clean. Also, check to see how firm the cake is in the center. When it's done, pull the cake off the coals, and let it cool in the Dutch oven. When it's cool, lift it out of the Dutch oven using the parchment.

Then serve it up!

EGGLESS, MILKLESS, BUTTERLESS CAKE

This cake is both yummy and simple. It also passes by the most unstable ingredients. It only uses one oven if you're going to serve it straight "from the Dutch," but if you want to pull it out, I'd recommend using a second Dutch oven for the batter, and lining the oven with parchment.

TOOLS
10-inch Dutch oven
15 coals under to boil
8–10 coals under to bake
16–18 coals above

INGREDIENTS
1 cup water
2 cups raisins
1 tsp. cinnamon
1 tsp. nutmeg
¼ tsp. salt
½ tsp. cloves
1 cup brown sugar
⅓ cup shortening

2 cups flour
1 tsp. baking soda
½ tsp. baking powder

START WITH lighting some coals. As the coals get white, set the Dutch oven on the coals with the water and other ingredients of the first set. Put the lid on and let it boil.

Once it's boiled for a few minutes, pull the Dutch oven off and uncover it to let it cool. Put the coals on the lid to keep it heated. After a few minutes of cooling, mix the flour and other dry ingredients together, and add them to the liquid. Stir it up well, and reset the coals over and under the oven.

This has a longer cook time than most cakes, so you'll end up replenishing the coals some. Keep extra fresh coals going by adding them to your active chimney or side fire. Bake the cake for 45 minutes to an hour.

OATMEAL CAKE

This recipe surprised me at first, but it's great. You're softening up the oatmeal before adding it to your cake batter, so there are two actual cooking steps. Three, if you include the mixing. Four, if you include the cooling and eating. That's the best step anyway, right?

TOOLS
8-inch Dutch oven
20–22 coals under to boil

12-inch Dutch oven
10–12 coals under to bake
22–24 coals above

CAKE
1 cup quick oats
1½ cups water

½ cups vegetable oil
1 cup brown sugar
1 cup white sugar

2 eggs
pinch of salt
1 tsp. cinnamon
1 tsp. baking soda
½ tsp. baking powder
1½ cups flour

ICING

½ cup butter
1 cup brown sugar
2 Tbsp. milk
1 cup shredded coconut
pinch of salt

½ cup chopped pecans or walnuts

START OFF like any other dish by getting the coals ready. Once you've got some white, set a lot of them under your smaller Dutch oven along with the water. Cover it up and let it get to boiling. Once it is, take it off the heat, add in the oats, stir it up, and let it sit and soak.

Add some fresh coals to the fire too.

While it's soaking and getting nice and soft, cream the oil and the sugars together. The purpose of this is to mix them, obviously, but more so it's to aerate the blend. The more air bubbles you have, the fluffier your cake will be. When I cream sugar and oils together, I usually use a slotted spoon. I've also used a potato masher. Blend it until it's creamy, until it looks and feels like a fluffed-up, whipped-up sugar.

Add in the eggs (fresh or reconstituted) one at a time, and keep blending and mushing while you do. Keep aerating. Next, add in the oatmeal mixture, a bit at a time. You're still blending through this process too. The next thing to blend in is the salt, cinnamon, baking soda, and baking powder. Finally, slowly add in the flour. Blend this whole mixture the same way you have been, using deep, pressured strokes to make sure that you're mashing any clumps of flour or other ingredients, and to get as much air in there as possible. As a final bit, run through it some with a hand blender too.

Then, prepare the 12-inch Dutch oven. Put a lot of coals on the lid, and set that aside to preheat. After about 10 minutes, wipe some oil on the bottom and sides of the pot, and cut a circle of parchment paper to lay across the bottom. Do you remember folding paper and cutting snowflakes? Well, do this, just don't cut all kinds of holes, but rather one cut to make it the right size for the bottom, then unfold it and put it in place. The oil will help hold it.

Pour the batter over it. Lay the bottom coals in a circle, and set the Dutch oven on the ring. Set the hot lid with the coals on top and mark the time.

About 10–15 minutes later, turn the Dutch oven on the coals about a quarter turn, and turn the lid as well. This will prevent hot spots from burning parts of your cake. At 30–35 minutes, check the cake. A toothpick, inserted and removed, should come out clean. If not, let it cook longer.

At about 10 minutes to the end of the baking, rinse out the 8-inch, and get it back over coals. Add the icing ingredients (except the nuts), and let it come to a boil. When it does, fold in the nuts and adjust the heat to just keep it hot, but not boiling.

When the cake is done, pour the hot icing over it, let it cool just a bit, and serve it straight from the Dutch oven.

The next few recipes involve apples, and, of course, the easiest way to store them is in dried form.

It's delicious to just munch them as they are, or they can be reconstituted with equal parts boiling water and apple chips (or chunks). Once they've been reconstituted, you could even puree them into applesauce.

If you take dried apples and run them through a blender, you get an apple powder, which can be used in place of sugar for sweetening. If you're considering using it in a recipe, keep in mind that it won't dissolve the same way sugar does.

FRIED APPLE PIE BITES

These are kind of like the small hand-held apple pie bits we used to get in the grocery store. They're great to make outdoors because you don't need plates to serve them. Just pick one up and start eating!

TOOLS
10-inch Dutch oven
15–20 coals under, for boiling or frying.

INGREDIENTS
4 cups dried apples
water to cover
1 cup granulated sugar
½ tsp. cinnamon
½ tsp. nutmeg
pinch of salt

2½ cups flour
3 tsp. baking powder
½ cup Crisco shortening
1½–2 cups ice water

Additional flour for mixing dough

About 1 cup Crisco shortening or other oil, for frying (enough to be ½–¾ inch deep in the bottom of the Dutch oven)

FIRST, WE'RE going to make the filling. I'll start off by lighting up some coals. If you have sliced dried apples, chop them up with a knife so you get cubes. I'll add those to the Dutch oven, and then put in enough water to cover the apples. I'll set that on the coals to boil. After it's boiled and reconstituted a bit, I'll add the sugar and flavorings to the pot to create a flavorful syrup. Once the apples are soft, sticky, and flavorful, I'll pull them off the coals, and put the apples and syrup into a separate bowl. Then I'll rinse out the Dutch oven (to be used again for the frying).

While the apples are boiling, I'll work on the crust dough. I'll mix the flour, baking powder, and Crisco, working it all together with a pastry cutter, or even my fingers. Then, I'll drizzle in the water a bit at a time, until it feels like a good pastry dough. It's hard to say exactly how much water that will be, since different flours will absorb different amounts of water.

Then, I'll take a small chunk, a little smaller than a golf ball, and roll it out into a small circle. I'll spread a tablespoon or two of the apple filling into the center and fold it over. With a wet fingertip, I'll moisten the edge of half of the crust, then close the other half over it. Press the air out from the middle, and then seal the edge. Repeat with remaining dough.

I'll set the Dutch oven back on the coals, replenished, with even more coals than before. I'll put in the oil. I'll let it take some time to melt and/or heat up. Once it's hot enough to crackle when a drop of water falls in, then it will be ready for the pies. I'll set three to four of them in the Dutch oven and let them cook until they're golden brown on each side. If you put in too many, it will cool the oil too much.

When they're done, I'll leave them out to cool on a paper towel. If you want, you can even sprinkle the crust with cinnamon sugar.

STEWED APPLES AND RAISINS

This is a delicious dessert, or even a breakfast treat!

TOOLS

8-inch Dutch oven
8–10 coals below

INGREDIENTS

4 cups water

1 cup dried apples
1 cup raisins
2 Tbsp. brown sugar (optional)
1–2 Tbsp. flour or cornstarch (optional, for thickening)

THIS IS a pretty simple dish. You start off with the small Dutch oven over coals, with the water set to boil (covered). Once it's boiling, add the dried apples and the raisins. Let it simmer uncovered for 10–15 minutes. If you like, you can add the brown sugar for additional sweetness and the flour to thicken the liquid. If you add the flour, take about a half cup of the hot liquid out of the Dutch oven (or as much as you can get), and then add a tablespoon of flour to that cup. Whisk it together so it's not clumpy, and then pour it back into the Dutch oven.

APPLESAUCE COOKIES

Traditional cookies don't usually work in a Dutch oven. There just isn't room. Typically, I like to make lots of cookies at once, so that there's more to eat, and it's all worth the work. In a traditional indoor oven, that's easy because you can spread the dough balls out on a large baking sheet. I suppose you could have a couple of heated 12-inch Dutch ovens going, and put 5–6 dough balls in each one, then pull them out to cool and do more. If you had a shallow 14-inch Dutch oven, that would help too, because there would be a larger flat surface area to bake the cookies.

I think that the easiest solution is to spread the dough out flat across the bottom of the Dutch oven in one really large cookie and serve it up sliced into bars.

TOOLS

12-inch shallow Dutch oven
20+ coals (to boil)

12 coals below (to bake)
16–18 coals above

INGREDIENTS

1 cup dehydrated applesauce
1 cup water (see below)

1 cup freeze-dried raisins
1½ cups boiling water

½ cup dehydrated shortening powder
about 2 tsp. water

¾ cup sugar
1 egg (or 2 Tbsp. whole egg powder + 3 Tbsp. water)

¼ tsp. salt
1 tsp. baking soda
2 cups flour
1 tsp. cinnamon
½ tsp. cloves

1 cup nuts

START BY lighting up some coals, and when they're getting white, put a 12-inch Dutch oven on, with 2–3 cups of water in it and the lid on. Let the water come to a boil. Then use that boiling water to pour over the applesauce and the dried raisins. Set them aside and let them reconstitute. Also, take a few minutes to reconstitute the dried shortening and egg, but use cold water for those.

Then, using a slotted spoon, mix the shortening and the sugar, and cream them together. Add in the egg, and then the applesauce. (It's possible, by the way, to make applesauce by powdering dried apple slices in a blender and then adding the boiling water.)

Next, add in all of the dry ingredients and stir them all together. Finally, mix in the raisins (drain them first) and nuts.

Set the heated coals on the lid of the Dutch oven to preheat. Empty the Dutch oven and dry it out. Spread just a little bit of cooking oil onto the bottom and sides. Dump the dough into the Dutch oven, and spread it out to the sides, making a flat disc.

Put the Dutch oven on the coals and top it with the preheated lid (now adjusted with the proper amount of coals both above and under). The lid needs to be preheated so that the cookie will be hit with a blast of heat right away, just like preheating your indoor oven. This will help activate the baking powder and help all the gas it's created to swell up. Let it bake for 10–12 minutes and check it. If it's done, then pull it off the coals and let it cool. Once it's cool, cut it into bars or wedges and enjoy a great dessert!

APPLE BROWN BETTY

TOOLS
12-inch Dutch oven
20+ coals below for boiling

12 coals below for baking
16–18 coals above

INGREDIENTS
3 cups water
4 cups dried apples

½ cup flour
½ tsp cinnamon
¼ cup oatmeal
¼ cup brown sugar
¼ cup clarified butter

TO DO this delicious dessert, I'll start by putting the Dutch oven on some hot coals, with the water, ready to boil. I'll put the lid on, and let it come to a boil.

While it's boiling, I'll mix the second set of items, stirring and cutting them all together in a bowl.

When the water boils, I'll add the dried apples, and stir them up. I'll take the Dutch oven off the coals and let the apples reconstitute for 5 or 10 minutes. Then I'll crumble the flour mix over the top of the apples, and set the lid back on.

I'll set the Dutch oven back on the heat, with the coals refreshed and configured for baking. I'll let it bake for 45 minutes to an hour. Then I'll serve it up!

CARROT CAKE

For some unknown and perverse reason, my oldest son dislikes chocolate cake. I know, I know, it's not natural, but there it is, nonetheless. So one of his favorite cakes is carrot cake.

Really, that's fine with me too. I love them both. Here's a recipe that you can make with shelf-stable ingredients.

TOOLS
10-inch Dutch oven
8–10 coals below
12–14 coals above

INGREDIENTS
2 cups flour
1¼ tsp. baking soda
½ tsp. salt
1 tsp. cinnamon
1 tsp. nutmeg
1 tsp. allspice

5 slices candied ginger, chopped
4 tsp. powdered egg whites
1 cup raisins

½ cup oil or clarified butter
1 cup sugar

1 (14.5-oz.) can sliced carrots

START THIS recipe by getting your coals hot. Once they're well lit, put about 12–14 coals on the Dutch oven's lid to preheat it. Then oil the inside of the Dutch oven. It's a good idea to line the bottom of the Dutch oven with a circle of parchment paper too, so the cake will lift out easily.

Then mix and whisk all of the powdered and dry ingredients in a bowl and set them aside.

With a stiff whisk or a slotted spoon, begin blending the oil and the sugar in another bowl. Whisk it or smoosh it with the spoon for several minutes so that the blend can become well aerated.

Then, using a fork, mash the carrots until they have a consistency like they had been shredded or grated. Keep the liquid that's in the can. Add the smashed carrots and the liquid into the bowl, and mix more. Then, gradually add in the powdered mix, stirring as you go. If, after mixing it all up, it still looks too dry, add water. Add with caution, however—just a drizzle at a time, while continuing to stir.

Finally, pour the batter over the parchment paper in the Dutch oven, and put it on the coals. Let it bake for 35–40 minutes, checking it from time to time with a toothpick or something similar.

When it's done, take it off the coals and let it cool, uncovered. When it's all cooled, you can invert the Dutch oven onto a small plate and remove the parchment. If you want, you can make another instance of this recipe and have a layer cake.

SHELF-STABLE BROWNIES

I love brownies! My wife likes them to be a bit more goopy, so when I make them for her, I cook them a little less. I like them a bit drier, so I cook them longer.

TOOLS
10-inch Dutch oven
8–10 coals below
12–14 coals above

INGREDIENTS
1½ cup flour
1 tsp. baking powder
½ cup cocoa powder
1½ cup sugar
½ tsp. salt
1 tsp. vanilla
3 tsp. powdered egg whites
⅔ cup oil
⅔ cup water
1 cup nuts, chopped (optional)
1 (16-oz.) bag chocolate chips (optional)

SIMILAR TO the previous cake recipe, the first thing I'll do when making these brownies is to get some coals hot, and preheat the lid of my Dutch oven. When using chemical leaveners like baking powder, it's important to start the cooking process with a good blast of hot air so that the gas bubbles in the batter immediately begin to expand.

Then, while the lid's heating, I'll prepare the Dutch oven. I'll coat the insides with oil and dust it with flour. If I'm planning on serving directly from the Dutch oven, that's all I'll do, but if I intend to pull the brownies out in their entirety, I'll also lay down a circle of parchment paper in the bottom of the Dutch oven.

I'll mix all of the ingredients in a bowl. I'll stir them really well, so most of the clumps are broken up. I also like chocolate chips in mine, but you don't have to add them. If you do use chips, hold about a quarter cup back in reserve.

Finally, I'll readjust the coals, and put the Dutch oven on the heat, with the lid on. I'll bake it for about 35–40 minutes, until it's the consistency I like (or my wife likes, usually).

How to Make a Dutch Oven Pie Crust

I'm honestly not a big pie baker. Not because I don't like them, of course, but because it takes a lot of work to really do it right, and I'm still learning that process. Still, I love the results! I've made apple pies, pumpkin pies, and, most recently, a pecan pie.

One thing I've noticed as I'm baking is that the crust is pretty much the same process in each pie I bake. So I'm thinking I should write that process out in it's own space, and then you'll be ready to do any pie recipe.

I used to make my pies in my 12-inch Dutch oven, but over time, I discovered that the 10-inch is better. The 12-inch is usually too much pie, and some ends up being spoiled.

Also, some people will bake their pies in pie tins, set inside a Dutch oven. That does make it easier to craft and easier to lift out. (However, current IDOS cook-off rules prohibit using any internal cooking devices like pans or trivets inside the Dutch ovens.) But I really like just baking right in the Dutch oven. I also like to serve it right from the Dutch too, so I'm not required to lift it out whole and complete. If you want to do that, it's not tough if you use the right trick.

But first, let's make the crust!

DUTCH OVEN PIE CRUST

TOOLS
10-inch Dutch oven

8–10 coals below
14–16 coals above

INGREDIENTS
1¼ cups shortening
3 cups flour
1 Tbsp. vinegar
5 Tbsp. water (chilled in ice)
1 egg (2 Tbsp. egg powder + 3 Tbsp. cold water)

I START simply by adding all of the ingredients into a large bowl. You can use butter or margarine, I'm told, instead of shortening, but those had other liquids in them, and they can make for less flaky crusts. I've always used all-purpose flour, because that's what I've always had on hand. You can use pastry flour if you want. It will have less protein, and so, less gluten.

I use a pastry cutter to mix the ingredients together. Blend them all, but don't knead, since you don't want to build any gluten in the flour. Also, working it less with my hands keeps it cool, so the fats don't melt.

Once it's mixed, I put it between two sheets of parchment or waxed paper and begin rolling. At this point, I'm not preparing it for the oven, but rather creating layers, so it can be rolled out quite thick. I dust it with just a little flour, and fold it in half, and then in quarters. Then, I roll it out again. A little more flour, a folding, and another rolling. I do that process 3–4 times, creating layers in the stack. Then I leave it in a clump, wrap it in plastic, and put it in the fridge to chill for a half hour or so.

In the meantime, I prepare the Dutch oven. I'll spray it with oil, lightly. Then, if I want to lift the pie out of the Dutch oven when it's done, I'll prepare the lifting mechanism. I'll cut two big squares of parchment. I fold these into two long strips and lay them across the bottom of the Dutch oven, folded up the sides, and over the edges. Then I cut a circle of parchment (you can use the lid as a template and cut it just a little smaller) and lay that in the Dutch oven, over the crossed strips of folded parchment.

Then it's time to roll out the dough. I take it out of the fridge and break off about two-thirds of it. I put it in between parchment or waxed paper sheets. I roll it out pretty thin, and cut it just smaller than the Dutch oven lid. I carefully lift the circle and the lower paper sheet and lightly fold it in half, with the paper on the inside. I set this down into the Dutch oven, then unfold it. Finally, I peel off the paper. It's tricky to position the dough after it's placed, so it's good to be careful as it's going in.

Then I take all of the leftover dough around the circle, and the extra that I broke away earlier, and I roll that out in a long rectangle. I cut that into strips, about 1–1¼ inches wide, and about 1 foot long.

Each of these strips are lifted up and placed around the inside side of the Dutch oven. I press them together and also press them into the "corner" where the bottom of the Dutch oven rises up into the wall. Presto! The crust is in place. Then I take a fork and poke holes in the bottom and the sides (to vent the steam).

In most cases, it's now ready for the filling. Make the pie happen! (One tip I heard when making fruit pies is to spread softened butter over the interior of the pie to keep the crust from soaking up much of the liquid in the filling.)

If my pie has a top crust, I'll roll out another amount of dough and cut another circle about the size of the lid. Using the same technique, I lift it onto the filling and position it, unfolding it, onto the top of the pie (after adding the filling, of course!). I'll pinch the sides and the top crust together in a decorative way and cut stylish vent holes in the top (usually 3–4) so the steam can release and keep the crust from tenting.

Then, I'll brush the top of the crust with a little milk and sprinkle some more sugar over the surface. This helps to make a nice sweet glaze.

DRIED APPLE PIE

Here's a great example of what can be done with the crust above.

TOOLS
8-inch Dutch oven
8–10 coals below

10-inch Dutch oven
8–10 coals below
12–14 coals above

INGREDIENTS
2½ cups or more of water
2½ cups dried apples

¾ cup sugar
¾ tsp. cinnamon
⅛ tsp. salt
raisins (optional)

2 tsp. clarified butter

BEFORE BAKING the pie, rehydrate the apples by heating the water to a boil in the 8-inch Dutch oven. Then, add the dried apples and let that sit for 5–10 minutes.

After the apples are soft, add the second set of ingredients to them. Make the crust as described above. Spread the clarified butter over the bottom crust before adding the apple and spice mix. Then close it off with the top crust and a little more butter and sugar, as desired.

When it's all assembled in the 10-inch Dutch oven, set it up on the coals for about 35–40 minutes, or until the top crust is browning and crisp. Then, take it off the coals and let it cool. Lift it out by the parchment handles, slice it up, and serve it!

A SURPRISING PINTO BEAN PIE

When I first heard of this, I was quite surprised. How can you make a pie out of beans? But it's great! I've also had brownies made of beans, so the concept wasn't totally foreign to me. Give it a try! This one will also use the crust method (see pages 106–107), but only a bottom crust.

TOOLS

10-inch Dutch oven
8–10 coals below
12–14 coals above

INGREDIENTS

½ cup sugar
1 cup brown sugar, packed
2 eggs (4 Tbsp. egg powder + 6 Tbsp. cold water)
½ cup clarified butter (or butter mixed from powder)

1 heaping cup cooked, mashed pinto beans (I use canned refried beans if they don't have additional flavorings).

START BY making the crust as shown in the previous recipe. Then heat up some coals.

To make the pie filling, mix the first set of ingredients together very well. Beat them with a stiff whisk or a slotted spoon. Do this for several minutes so as to aerate the mixture. Then, add the pinto beans.

Cut or fold them into the mix at first, and then stir and beat them with as much vigor as you can. When that's smooth, empty the bowl into the pie crust.

Put the Dutch oven on the coals as listed for baking, and let it bake for 40–45 minutes. You may have to replenish the coals toward the end of the baking time. Remember to turn the Dutch oven every 15 minutes, and to turn the lid so as to prevent hot spots and burn spots.

Use a fork to test the center, and when it comes out clean, it's done! Let it cool and serve it up!

Here are a couple of recipes for whipped toppings to go nicely onto the pies and brownies!

THE FIRST WHIPPED TOPPING

INGREDIENTS

1 cup ice cold water
1 cup powdered milk
1 cup powdered sugar

MIX THE ingredients together and beat with a whisk for a long time, until your arms fall off, or you get to the right consistency—whichever happens first!

THE SECOND WHIPPED TOPPING

INGREDIENTS
6 Tbsp. instant dry milk
1 cup hot water

2 tsp. unflavored gelatin
2 Tbsp. cold water

2–4 Tbsp. sugar
1 tsp. vanilla

START BY mixing the milk in the hot water, and the gelatin in the cool water. Once each of those is nicely dissolved, combine those two, and chill the mixture until it gels. Once it's gelled, add the vanilla and sugar. Using a whisk, whip it until it's like whipped topping. That could take a while, but it will be worth it! Pies are always better with something creamy on top, right?

CHAPTER 4

SIDES

IT'S ALWAYS good to have a variety on your plate, right? When planning a meal, it's a good idea to have a main dish and one or two sides, maybe a bread. Here are some great side dishes that have been made with shelf-stable ingredients.

MAKE YOUR OWN CRACKED WHEAT

One of my favorite sides with Chinese food is ham-fried rice. The concept is simple. Take cooked rice, some cooked eggs and veggies, and brown them up in a skillet with some seasonings.

The difference here is that instead of using rice, you're using cracked wheat. Now, it's important to know that these recipes use true cracked wheat, not bulgur. The two are not the same, even though they're both wheat that has been cracked. Bulgur is pre-cooked and processed differently.

Cracked wheat can be purchased, but since the wheat berries are broken open, the oils will begin to oxidize, causing it to go bad after time. It's not a bad idea to make your own as you need it. Cracked wheat can be made by setting your wheat grinder to a very, very coarse setting or chopping the wheat up in a blender. Once that's done, you use a strainer to sift out the flour powder, leaving the big cracked chunks of wheat.

CHINESE FRIED WHEAT

TOOLS

10-inch Dutch oven
15–16 coals below

8-inch Dutch oven (for optional gravy)
8–10 coals below

INGREDIENTS

4 cups water

¼ cup dehydrated onion
¼ cup dehydrated celery
1 cup bacon- or ham-flavored TVP

1 cup cracked wheat (strain out flour before cooking)
½ tsp. salt

3 Tbsp. vegetable oil
1 beaten egg (2 Tbsp. egg powder + 3 Tbsp. cold water)

2 Tbsp. soy sauce or to taste

THERE ARE a number of steps to this dish. Each of the ingredients must be prepared and then fried together.

Once the coals are ready, get the 10-inch Dutch oven on them with the water and the lid on. Let it boil, then dip out 1½ cups. Mix that boiling water with the first set of ingredients, the dehydrated veggies and meat.

Put the cracked wheat and the salt in with the still-boiling water and let it cook for 20 minutes or so, until the wheat is soft. Put the wheat into a strainer and drain off the liquid (keep the liquid, though, if you want a gravy). If you can, rinse the wheat in cold water. That will make the grains fluffier and also stop the cooking process. Press out all the extra water from both the wheat and the rehydrated veggies and meat.

While that's draining, wipe out the 10-inch Dutch oven and put it back on the coals. Add the oil or clarified butter and let it heat up.

Pour in the egg and scramble it or let it cook flat. When it's done, scoop it out, cut it into pieces, and add it to the wheat mixture. Add the reconstituted ingredients to the wheat mixture as well, and stir.

Add more oil to the Dutch oven and let it heat back up. Replenish the coals if it's needed. Then, pour everything back into the Dutch oven and let it fry, stirring occasionally, and adding the soy sauce liberally, to taste. If you have some dried Thai chiles, those would add in nicely as well.

If you want gravy, take any leftover liquid from the wheat and veggies, and add it into the 8-inch Dutch oven. Put that on coals and let it start to simmer. Add in soy sauce and pepper to taste. There's really no need for salt if you're using soy sauce. Whisk some flour and water together and drop it by teaspoon into the gravy to find the right thickness without clumping.

And there's a wonderful side dish.

SLOW-COOKED BBQ PINTO BEANS

This is a delicious comfort food that reminds me of summer and picnics. The more comfortable you can feel when in a stressful situation, the better, right? This will be a longer simmer, so the temperature is slightly lower.

TOOLS

12-inch Dutch oven
18–20 coals below

INGREDIENTS

2 cups pinto beans
5 cups water

1/2 cup dehydrated onions
1/2 cup dehydrated sweet peppers
1/2 cup bacon-flavored TVP

1 Tbsp. chili powder
3/4 cup BBQ sauce
1/2 cup ketchup
1 1/2 Tbsp. mustard

TO MAKE this dish, you have several options. First, if you use beans directly from the bag, you're going to be cooking a long, long time. I mean, like, hours. That's okay if you've got that time to manage the coals. Maybe you're cooking other things as well, so you'll be there anyway.

A second option is to soak the beans in water overnight. If you do this, you'll cut the cooking time by over half. But you do have to think ahead. If you do this, make sure that you fill the bowl with the beans and with enough water to cover the beans by about 2 inches or more. Then there'll be plenty of water for the beans to absorb.

A third option is to use canned beans. This is the fastest. If you do this, reduce the water by 2 cups.

The first step, after getting coals hot, is to get the beans and the water boiling, with the Dutch oven lid on. After that, I'll watch it, replenishing the coals until the beans are cooked through. When I cook beans, I usually use method 2, and it usually takes about an hour to an hour and a half for them to get soft after they have soaked overnight. To test them, just eat a few. If it's crunchy, it's not done.

Then, I'll mix all of the dehydrated ingredients into a bowl and spoon in 2 cups of the boiling beany water. I'll let that sit to fully hydrate for at least 15 minutes.

At some point, the beans will be done and the extras will be well-hydrated. I'll drain the beans and any extra water in the bowl and combine them both into the Dutch oven. I'll add in all of the third set of ingredients and mix it all up. Taste it and see if it tastes right to you. Adjust any of the flavorings to taste, with salt, too, if it's needed (the BBQ sauce will already have some and the mustard and ketchup will bring tang from vinegar).

Then I'll put it back on the coals for another 15–30 minutes to bring it all up to temperature and mix the flavors more. Then serve!

CURRIED LENTILS WITH RICE

I love curry! One of my favorite dishes with it is masaman curry, which includes potatoes, coconut, and peanut butter. I like both hot and mild curry. It's just great! One thing that's cool about curry, too, is that it can be used as a side dish or it can even be a main dish. I really like meat in my curries, so if you wanted to add a can of chicken breast to this, you could. The lentils, however, do make it quite hearty.

This recipe has multiple steps. First, you cook the lentils. Then, while you're cooking the curry, you're also cooking the rice.

TOOLS
8-inch Dutch oven
10 coals below (to start)

10-inch Dutch oven
12–15 coals below

INGREDIENTS
2 cups water
2 cups green or brown lentils

2 cups chicken-flavored broth
¼ cup dehydrated onions
½ cup dehydrated carrot dices
1 cup dehydrated tomatoes

½ cup "rich" milk (3 Tbsp. powdered milk mixed with ½ cup water)
2 Tbsp. sour cream powder
½ tsp. garlic powder
1 tsp. (or more) curry powder, to taste
salt
pepper
paprika

1½ cups rice
3 cups water

FIRST, I'LL get some hot coals under my 8-inch Dutch oven with the water and the lentils. I'll put the lid on and let that come up to a simmer. I'll check it so that it's a gentle simmer and adjust the coals to make that happen. After 20–25 minutes, the lentils should be cooked. I'll take a bite to see and if they're soft, then they're ready.

Then I'll get some hot coals under my 10-inch Dutch oven (the cooking can overlap) and start to heat up the broth with the lid on. That can be actual chicken broth, from a can, or it can be with bouillon cubes. Whatever ya got!

When there's a good simmer going on in the 10-inch Dutch oven, I'll add the dehydrated ingredients and let them reconstitute, stirring as I go. Then, I'll add in the milk, sour cream, and other seasonings. Once the lentils are cooked, I'll drain them (holding onto a half cup or so of the water) and add them into the 10-inch Dutch oven with the other ingredients. Use the extra water to add to the 10-inch to get the curry to the consistency you like, more or less runny. Finally, I'll close the lid and let it simmer for another 20 minutes or so.

A note about the curry powder. Many commercial curry powders are mild and some are hot. Unless you know what you're dealing with, go cautiously and err on the side of too little curry. Taste along the way and add more until it tastes right. You can't remove heat, but you can always add more in.

Once the curry is simmering away, rinse out the 8-inch Dutch oven and put it back on the coals with the rice and water, covered. Watch for it to start boiling, and let it go for about 10 minutes. Then, take it off the coals and let it sit, covered, for another 10 minutes or so. The rice should be just about perfectly cooked that way.

Finally, serve up the rice with the curry on top!

BROWN SUGAR GLAZED CARROTS

This is a very quick and easy side dish that's quite traditional in Dutch oven circles. I think it works best if the carrots are in bigger chunks, but, as always, use what you have.

TOOLS
8-inch Dutch oven
10 coals below

INGREDIENTS
2½ cups water
1 cup dehydrated carrots

2 Tbsp. dehydrated butter (or use clarified butter)
1 cup brown sugar
salt
pepper

THE PROCESS for this recipe is as easy as it gets. Start with some hot coals and put your Dutch oven on with the water, covered. When the water boils, add in the carrots. Let them simmer for about 15 minutes until the carrots are tender. Then drain off the water.

Add in the butter, sugar, and salt and pepper to taste. Stir and cook it until the sugar dissolves into the residual liquid and the butter. If you don't have any brown sugar, by the way, you can use regular sugar and a tablespoon of molasses.

SCALLOPED POTATOES

TOOLS
10-inch Dutch oven
15+ coals below (for boiling the water)

8 coals below (for finishing)
12 coals above

INGREDIENTS
4–5 cups water
2 cups dehydrated potato slices
¼ cups dehydrated onion

2 tsp. salt
1 tsp. pepper
1 (10.75-oz.) can cream of mushroom soup
⅓ cup powdered milk

½ cup freeze-dried cheddar (optional)

THIS IS a pretty simple dish as well. Once I've got the coals hot, I'll put a lot of them under the Dutch oven and add the water to boil, covered. When that's boiling, I'll add in the potatoes and the onion.

I'll let that simmer for a few minutes, and then add the ingredients in the next set. Then I'll reset the coals in the baking configuration and let it cook for 20–25 minutes. If you have the cheddar, reconstitute it, and sprinkle it on top after about 15 minutes of cooking.

MATZO BALLS (JEWISH DUMPLINGS) IN CHICKEN SOUP

I'm not fully familiar with the Jewish traditions, but during the Passover week in early spring, the faithful don't eat leavened bread. Passover is the celebration of the time when the destroying angel "passed over" the children of Israel while they were in slavery in Egypt and instead killed the firstborn of the Egyptians. It was the final plague that convinced the pharaoh to let the children of Israel go. Even though it's a celebration, it also remembers a very sad and difficult time in their history. So they eat a lot of bitter herbs and refrain from leavened bread.

Now, even for the Gentiles, Jewish tradition has brought some delicious foods. And even if it doesn't have the religious significance, it's great comfort food!

TOOLS
12-inch Dutch oven
20+ coals below

INGREDIENTS
1 cup cracker crumbs (matzo or even just saltines or soda crackers)
4 eggs (8 Tbsp. egg powder + 12 Tbsp. cool water)
4 Tbsp. oil
1 tsp. garlic powder
1 tsp. salt

8–9 cups water
2–3 cubes chicken bouillon

½ cup dehydrated onion
½ cup dehydrated peppers
1 (12.5-oz.) can chicken breast
salt
pepper

THIS DISH is different because it starts out long before I light the coals! I'll start by mashing up the crackers. Now, you can go out and buy actual matzo crackers or you can (if you're not orthodox) just make this with saltines/soda crackers or just about any kind of cracker you want. I wonder if the baking soda technically counts as leavening in the Jewish code. Hmmm . . . I don't know! In any case, the crackers should be mashed up very fine. In fact, if you have access to power, you could use a blender to get the crumbs as fine as possible.

Then I'll rehydrate the eggs and add them into the bowl with the crackers, along with the oil and seasonings. I'll mash that all together with my hands and let it chill somehow (fridge, ice cooler, or whatever else you have access to) for about an hour or more.

During that time, I can gather the other ingredients and get some coals glowing! I'll set the Dutch oven on the coals and pour in the water. I'll add the bouillon cubes and put on the lid to let it boil.

Once it's heated and boiling, I'll add in the last set of ingredients and let it boil again, covered. By this time, the matzo mix should be chilled enough. I'll retrieve it and form it into small balls, just smaller than a golf ball, and drop them into the boiling broth. Then, I'll reclose the lid and let it cook, simmering, for another 20 minutes or so.

Then, soup's on!

MACARONI AND CHEESE

Hey. C'mon. Who doesn't like mac an' cheese? Really? It's what we've all been eating since we were kids. I'll bet each of you has a favorite way of fixing it too! Mine was to make it up and add a drained can of tuna. I also liked to melt shredded cheddar on top of it. It's really simple to make too.

TOOLS

8-inch Dutch oven
10–12 coals below

INGREDIENTS

at least 3 cups water
1 tsp. salt
2 cup macaroni

¼ powdered milk mixed with ½ cup hot water
½ cup butter powder mixed with 6 Tbsp. cool water (or ½ cup clarified butter)
⅓ cup cheese powder

⅓ cup reconstituted cheddar cheese (optional)

I'LL START by heating the coals and getting some under my 8-inch Dutch oven. I'll add the water and the salt and let it boil. Keeping the lid on will help it to boil faster. Once it's boiling, I'll add the macaroni and let it keep boiling with the lid still on.

It should be done in about 10 minutes. I'll test a piece or two to make sure. I like my pasta "al dente," which means it's soft but not smooshy; it still resists my teeth a little bit.

When it's done, I'll drain it, saving the water. I'll use some of that water to mix the milk. I'll also use cool water to reconstitute the butter if I'm not using clarified butter. Then I'll add the remaining ingredients, stirring them into the macaroni. Stir well, until all of the powders dissolve and the sauce becomes creamy.

Finally, you can add the cheddar (if you have it) to the top, put some coals on the lid, and let it sit for 5–10 more minutes until the cheese melts. Then serve it up next to your main dish!

REFRIED BEANS, FROM A HOMEMADE MIX

Refried beans make a great side for any Mexican or southwestern dish. I love to serve them up with Spanish rice and some chile verde and tortillas. Actually, that just made me want Mexican food . . .

I've doubled the original recipe I found so that you can make more and keep it on hand.

TOOLS
8-inch Dutch oven
10 coals below

INGREDIENTS
3 cups pinto or black bean flour
1 tsp. cumin
3 tsp. chili powder
3 tsp. salt
¼ tsp. garlic powder (optional)
2 tsp. instant minced onions (optional)

2½ cups water
¾ cups bean mixture
1 cup salsa (optional)

THE FIRST thing is to make the bean flour. This is done by grinding up the kind of beans you like (for southwest, I like pinto or black beans, or both). This can be done in a blender or in a hand grinder.

Second, mix all of the powdered ingredients in a zip-top baggie and shake it all up.

Then, when it's time to cook, heat the water to a boil in the 8-inch Dutch oven, covered, on about 10 coals. Add in the bean mixture and, if you have it, the salsa. Stir and let it cook on the coals for about 5 minutes or so. It will thicken more and more as it cools.

Serve it up next to your favorite burrito or even add it to the inside of the burrito!

SMOTHERED GREEN BEANS

Sometimes, when I've been working on a really fancy dinner in my Dutch ovens or the main dish is really complex, I want to do a side, but I don't want a lot of fuss. Plus, if you do a really fancy side, sometimes it detracts from the impact of the main dish or the dessert.

Often I'll just heat up some canned veggies. I usually like to mix them up a bit, like maybe some green beans and some corn. Here, however, is a great way to kick this side up a notch without too much extra work.

TOOLS

10-inch Dutch oven
15 coals below

INGREDIENTS

2 Tbsp. clarified butter, margarine, or butter flavor Crisco
2 (14.5-oz.) cans cut green beans
1 (3-oz.) jar Hormel bacon real bacon bits
1 (2-oz.) pkg. onion soup mix
salt
pepper
garlic powder

START OFF with the Dutch oven on some heated coals and melt the butter/shortening on the bottom of the oven. Then add one drained can of beans and one can with the liquid. Add in the bacon bits and the onion soup mix. Also, add the salt, pepper, and garlic powder to taste. Stir them all together and cook until the liquid reduces and the flavorings coat the beans.

BBQ LIMA BEANS

This is a delicious dish to go alongside meat or potatoes, though it does take awhile to cook. It has a rich, sweet, and tangy taste!

TOOLS

12-inch Dutch oven
20+ coals below (for boiling the beans)
10–12 coals below (for the baking)
16–18 coals above

INGREDIENTS
2 cups large dried lima beans
8 cups water
1 (3-oz.) jar Hormel bacon real bacon bits

1/4 cup dehydrated onion
1 tsp. garlic powder
1/2 cup margarine or clarified butter
1 tsp. prepared mustard
2 tsp. Worcestershire sauce
1 1/2 tsp. chili powder
1 (8-oz.) can tomato sauce
2 Tbsp. brown sugar
2 Tbsp. vinegar

THE FIRST step in this dish is to light up the coals and boil the water in the Dutch oven with the lid on. Once it is boiling, I'll add in the beans and the bacon bits and let it simmer until the beans are soft. That could be as long as an hour and a half.

Once the beans are done, I'll drain them and hold back about a 1/2 cup of the water.

Then, I'll put the Dutch oven back on the coals and melt the butter/margarine. I'll add in the other ingredients and let the flavors all merge. Finally, I'll add in the lima beans and bacon and cover it back up. I'll readjust the coals for baking and cook it for another 1 1/2 to 2 hours. Obviously, you'll need to keep a side fire and replenish your coals occasionally. Use the bean liquid if you have to keep it at the right consistency.

CHAPTER 5

BREAKFAST

I THINK that I was cursed early on with a physiological inability to sleep in. If the sun comes up, I'm up with it.

That's okay, though, because that means that I often get the chance (even while camping) to make a really good breakfast. Sure, you can rip open a box or a bag of cereal (and I often do), or smear some Philly on a bagel, but once in a while, it's great to really have a breakfast, cooked and hearty. And even in times of crisis, it's good to have good food, especially early in the morning.

When I think of breakfast, the first things I think of are pancakes and waffles. To do that, let's use the Basic Master Mix recipe from the Breads chapter! I've included it here, for quick reference.

BASIC MASTER MIX RECIPE

20 cups flour
2½ cups powdered milk (unmixed—still a powder)
¾ cup double acting baking powder

3 Tbsp. salt
2 Tbsp. cream of tartar
½ cup sugar

1 lb. vegetable shortening or reconstituted shortening powder

FIRST, SIFT or whisk all of the first set of ingredients together. Mix it well, because the entire quantity needs to be an even balance of all of the ingredients.

Then, use a pastry cutter to cut in the shortening until it looks well blended, like cornmeal. You can even use your hands to work out some of the bigger chunks.

Once it's all mixed, store it in larger zip-top bags or another airtight container in a cool, dry place. It keeps well for 6–8 weeks. You can use it in your recipes. Another way to keep it longer is to mix larger quantities with everything but the fats and to make smaller batches from that (oil added) for more frequent, temporary use. You can store the smaller quantities in the zip-top bags as well.

Instead of making biscuits with this mix, we're going to make pancakes.

PANCAKES

TOOLS
12-inch Dutch oven lid, on a trivet
22+ coals underneath

INGREDIENTS
3 cups basic master mix
1 egg from powder (2 Tbsp. whole egg powder + 3 Tbsp. water)
1½ cups water (adjust to the consistency you like)

START OFF by getting the coals hot and putting them in a circle on your cooking surface. Then, put a Dutch oven lid stand or a trivet over the coals. If you don't have one, you can use a few standard-size masonry bricks (the kind and size that a brick house is made of) set to the side of the coals. Turn a Dutch oven lid upside down and put it on the trivet, bricks, or even rocks, over the coals. The idea is for the lid to rest about an inch or so above the coals, maybe even a half inch. The inverted lid will become your griddle.

You can use a Dutch oven itself as a skillet, but the high sides of the oven make it hard to get a spatula underneath and flip the pancakes.

Put just a bit of oil on the lid and let it get hot. You could use clarified butter (see page 32) for this, which will enrich the taste of the final pancakes!

While the lid is heating, mix the ingredients. Reconstitute the egg (or eggs, if you're doubling), add the water, and mix it up. A suggestion: wetter, thinner batter makes for thinner pancakes that cook better, in my opinion. Thicker pancakes are harder to judge and harder to flip. Some people also like to use milk to mix pancakes. I do! Keep in mind, though, that there *is* milk in the mix, so don't feel too bad if you don't have more to add in. There are also a lot of variant ingredients you can add at this point, but I'll talk about those in a minute.

Then, begin cooking the pancakes on your lid griddle. Here are some things to remember:

Cook the first side until the bubbles don't fill back in. This has been a standard way for many years of telling if a pancake is done. It's a little tricky because a pancake is usually thicker in the middle than the edges. If your Dutch oven lid is concave instead of flat, that will be even more so. Still, watch the pancake until most bubbles are forming, popping, and not filling back in. That means that the batter underneath the bubbles is setting and cooking.

Only flip once. If you've timed it right, the pancake will only need a few moments to cook on the second side.

Heat control is important to great pancakes. If it's too cool, it will take forever to cook and the pancakes won't really cook right. If it's too hot, the first side will be really dark by the time the bubbles are staying popped. Cooking outside with coals makes it even trickier because of so many variables. Just be ready to pull out 3–4 coals or to slip in 2–3 more coals. Your first couple of pancakes might not be as well adjusted as the rest.

When you serve up the pancakes, syrup is pretty shelf-stable. However, if you have no syrup, what do you do? One option is to make some of your own by mixing sugar and water and boiling it down. This can take a very long time, and it's tricky to get the right consistency. I simply prefer to use honey.

VARIATIONS

I like to add a few shakes of cinnamon and nutmeg to my pancakes. Plus, I like to sweeten the basic master mix a little with some honey or extra sugar.

Dried apples can add a fruity taste. You can reconstitute them first, or just add them in. Again, I like cinnamon and nutmeg with apples. You can really add just about any dehydrated fruit. Most prepackaged blueberry muffins are actually flavored with colored dried apples, not blueberries.

My wife taught me just how wonderful it is to have pancakes and waffles with peanut butter.

WAFFLES

To make waffles, use the same recipe (some will add in the equivalent of an extra egg for additional lift and fluff). Cooking waffles outdoors can be tricky because you need a special iron, and you can't really do it in an ordinary Dutch oven. There are companies that make cast iron waffle irons that you can use over coals or a campfire. I have found that it's important to make sure that they are consistently well oiled (the clarified butter or the mixed shortening would work) for each waffle.

Our family has a tradition of swirling (not mixing) odd food coloring combinations through the batter. It doesn't change the flavor or anything, but it looks cool. We call them "awfuls" instead of "waffles."

BERRY BREAKFAST BARS

The oats and flours in this delicious dish will give everyone a hearty and filling breakfast. It's good for camping and snacking as well.

TOOLS
8-inch Dutch oven
10 coals below

12-inch Dutch oven
12–14 coals below
22–26 coals above

INGREDIENTS
2 cups freeze-dried berries
1 cup water
2½ Tbsp. cornstarch
1 Tbsp. lemon juice

1 cup white flour
1 cup whole wheat flour
2 cups quick rolled oats
1 cup brown sugar
1¼ tsp. baking powder
¾ tsp. salt
½ tsp. ground allspice
1 cup butter or margarine

THE FIRST task in preparing this is to get some coals lit. As they burn and start to turn white, remember to toss them in the chimney or stir the stack so that they all get evenly lit. As soon as you can, get some coals under the 8-inch Dutch oven with the water in it. This is not to boil, but you do want it to get quite hot so it will reconstitute the berries. Add the berries when the water is hot.

When they're reconstituted, remove them and add the cornstarch and lemon juice to the remaining liquid. Stir it and keep it cooking until it's thick, like a syrup. Then pull it off the coals and mix the berries back in. Set that aside. You'll probably also want to replenish your coals for the next step. Also, set a lot of coals onto the lid of your 12-inch Dutch oven to preheat.

Then whisk together the dry ingredients in a mixing bowl. Cut in the butter with a pastry cutter or table knives until it all looks crumbly.

Grease or oil the interior of your 12-inch Dutch oven (maybe even line it with parchment paper). Then press in ⅔ of the crumb mixture. Spread it evenly. Put the lid on and adjust the coals above and below, as shown above. Let it bake for 15–20 minutes until it's nicely golden.

Then take the berry mixture and spread it over the crust you've made. Scatter the remaining crumb mixture on top of the berries and put it back on to bake for another 15–20 minutes.

When it's all nicely browned, pull it off the coals and let it cool, uncovered. Slice it into bars or triangles and serve them up! For slicing, by the way, I find those curved Alaskan blades to be very useful. I can press in from the top and get into the corners. If you don't have one, any knife will do.

BREAKFAST TACOS

This one is really easy and could be used nicely for camping as well as for saving your life at the end of the world as we know it. It goes in two steps—reconstituting all of the dried ingredients and cooking them up and serving them!

TOOLS

12-inch Dutch oven
20+ coals underneath

INGREDIENTS

4 cups water (to heat and for cold reconstitution).
1 Tbsp. clarified butter
1 cup cooked freeze dried potato dices
1 cup bacon- or taco-flavored textured vegetable protein (TVP)
4 eggs (8 Tbsp. whole egg powder + 12 Tbsp. water)

4 (8-inch) flour tortillas
¾ cup freeze dried cheddar cheese
½ cup thick and chunky salsa

WHEN MAKING these tacos, I'll start off by heating up the coals and getting them under my Dutch oven. I'll add in 4 cups water and let it heat or even boil. Then, in separate bowls, I'll rehydrate the potatoes and the TVP.

While those are soaking, I'll wipe out the Dutch oven and get it back on the coals to dry off. I'll also take this opportunity to mix the eggs and to rehydrate the cheese using cold water.

As the Dutch oven heats up again, I'll add in the clarified butter (which you can make according to the instructions on page 32). Then, in go the potatoes for browning and sautéing. Once they have a nice brown edge, I'll add in the TVP and allow it to brown as well. Finally, the eggs go in, and I'll stir it all as they cook and set.

As the eggs are finishing, I'll drape the tortillas, one at a time, over the mix in the Dutch oven to warm up and soften. Then, I'll serve a bit of the egg mix in the middle of the tortilla, add a bit of the cheese and salsa, and we'll all dig in!

LOADED POTATO BREAKFAST CASSEROLE

TOOLS
12-inch Dutch oven

20+ coals under (for boiling water)

10–12 coals under (for baking)
16–18 coals above

INGREDIENTS
5–6 cups water
4 cups dried potatoes, in cubes or shreds
½ cup dried green onions
½ cup freeze-dried red bell peppers, reconstituted
¾ cup freeze-dried textured vegetable protein (TVP), bacon
1 cup powdered sour cream, reconstituted with 2 cups water
2 cups freeze-dried cheddar cheese
1 packet (up to 1 oz.) ranch dip/dressing mix

ONCE THE coals are getting a little white, I'll put the water in the Dutch oven and set it, covered, on the coals to boil. Once it's boiling, I'll ladle some of the water out into a bowl with the dehydrated onions, peppers, and bacon. I'll use just enough water to get them reconstituted.

In the Dutch oven, with the rest of the water, I'll add the dried potatoes. I cover that back up and let them rehydrate and cook. In the meantime, I'll use cold water to reconstitute the sour cream and the cheese.

Once the potatoes are done and soft, I'll add the remaining ingredients in to the Dutch oven and reset the coals for baking above and below. You might need to add some fresh coals. I'll bake it 45 minutes or so, until it's nicely brown and bubbly.

HONEY-NUT GRANOLA

I've tried lots of different granolas over the years. I've really liked almost all of them, but some more than others. This one's good, and you can adjust it to whatever you like. You can add different nuts for different flavors or different dried fruits. Just use what you have!

TOOLS
12-inch Dutch oven
10–12 coals below
16–18 coals above

INGREDIENTS
½ cup vegetable oil
½ cup honey
½ cup brown sugar
½ cup crunchy peanut butter

4 cups quick oats
¾ cup sliced almonds
¾ cup shredded coconut
¾ cup wheat germ
¾ cup dried fruit (optional)

TO MAKE this, I will do things a little differently. Usually, I'll get the coals ready, put the food into the Dutch oven, and put it on the coals. In this case, I'll put an empty, oiled Dutch oven onto the coals (top and bottom) and then add the food to the preheated oven.

So, once the coals are ready and the Dutch oven is preheating, mix the first set of ingredients together. Stir them up well, though with the honey and the peanut butter that will take some work. Use a wooden or metal spoon.

Then, in a larger bowl, mix the second set of ingredients, along with whatever other nuts or things you want to include. If you use dried fruit, chop them up into tiny bits, because they won't rehydrate and get soft in the cooking.

Then, mix the two mixtures together and dump the whole thing into the preheated Dutch oven. Every ten minutes or so, open it up and give it a stir—partly to prevent burning and partly to keep it broken into smaller chunks. After about a half hour, dump it out onto a parchment paper and spread it around. Break it up into bite-sized chunks. Let it cool, and break it up further, if you need to. Then store it in a zip-top baggie. When it's breakfast time, enjoy it with milk, or just munch it as a snack.

TVP BREAKFAST MEAL

Hot cereals were always on my "yuck" list as a kid. To me, the name "mush" was perfect for them. The flavors were okay, I guess, because we layered them with brown sugar and other sweeteners, but it was always the textures that I found disgusting.

Then, as I grew up, I discovered that there were a lot of different ways to cook things and a wide variety of flavorings. I learned that the textures weren't that bad. I learned to like them! Just like I learned to like asparagus, broccoli, and even brussels sprouts.

So, here's a fun one that's made with all shelf-stable ingredients. Even though this recipe is a good hearty breakfast for two, this can be easily doubled for more servings.

TOOLS
8-inch Dutch oven
8–10 coals below

INGREDIENTS
2 cups water
¾ cup textured vegetable protein (TVP), unflavored)

¾ cup rolled oats
1 Tbsp. sugar
1 tsp. molasses
1 tsp. vanilla
1 tsp. cinnamon
6 Tbsp. pecans

WITH SOME hot coals, I'll add all of the ingredients to the Dutch oven and put it on the coals, covered. Once it's boiling, I'll pull a couple of coals and take off the lid so it calms to a good simmer and let it cook down a bit for 10–15 minutes. This will make a drier, more dense mush. If you like yours to be looser, put the lid back on, trapping the moisture within. When this is served, it really doesn't need much by way of toppings. You could add dried fruits if you wanted, but the molasses delivers a rich, deep sweetness that I really like.

TVP BREAKFAST SAUSAGE

I love sausage. It's probably one of my all-time favorite meats. I like lots of different kinds of sausage as well, including brats, summer sausage, hot Italian sausage, and lots more.

I love breakfast sausage, as patties or links. I'll usually eat a patty on a bagel or a bun with a slice of cheese. I also like it with scrambled egg. You can cook scrambled eggs without a lot of scraping and stirring (scrambling) and it turns out as a kind of flat pancake, which you can fold and cut into shape and put on the bagel too.

TOOLS

8-inch Dutch oven
8–10 coals below

12-inch Dutch oven
22+ coals below

INGREDIENTS

1½ cups water
½ tsp. cumin
1 tsp. sage
1 tsp. poultry seasoning (or 1 tsp. Italian seasoning)
½ tsp. red pepper flakes (or more to taste)

½ tsp. garlic powder
1 tsp. paprika
1½ tsp. salt
½ tsp. black pepper
1–3 drops liquid smoke flavoring
½ tsp. sugar

1 cup textured vegetable protein (TVP)
4 Tbsp. egg powder
1 Tbsp. vital wheat gluten
2 Tbsp. flour

1–2 Tbsp. oil

TO MAKE this wonderful sausage substitute, I'll begin with the 8-inch Dutch oven over some hot coals. I'll add in the water and all of the flavorings and seasonings. I'll stir that up and cover it to help it come to a boil.

While I'm waiting, I'll mix the second set of ingredients together. When the liquid boils, I'll pour it into the bowl with the dry ingredients. Once it's stirred up, it should have the consistency of ground meat. If not, I'll add a little flour if it's too wet or water if it's too dry. Add small amounts, then mix it and reassess, since it's easy to overshoot.

I'll roll the mix into balls about the size of golf balls. At that point, I have some choices: fry it immediately, make meatballs, or use it later, crumbled up in another dish.

If I'm going to use it right away, I'll get my 12-inch Dutch oven over about 22+ coals with 1–2 tablespoons of oil in the bottom. I'll let it heat up quite a bit. I'll flatten the balls into patties and fry them until they're brown and crisp on each side. Then, I'll serve it up on a bagel like I suggested earlier!

If I'm going to make pasta and meatballs, for example, I'll still oil and heat up the 12-inch Dutch oven, but I'll put 10–12 coals underneath and 16–18 coals above and add the meatballs inside. I'll bake them that way for about 20 minutes until they hold their shape. The bottom will brown, so after 10 minutes, I'll open it up and turn them.

If I'm going to use it later, I'll flatten it out onto the bottom of the 12-inch Dutch oven and set that on the same coals as the meatballs (with or without preheating). In about 20 minutes it should feel pretty solid. I'll put that big patty into a zip-top baggie, and then crumble it for lasagna or whatever I want.

Options, options, options!

OATMEAL RAISIN MUFFINS

Making muffins in a Dutch oven is tricky. The big problem is keeping them in the shape of a cup without them flattening out in the baking. There are two ways of fixing this problem. One is to use the metal foil cake cups instead of paper. These will be stiff enough to hold the cake upright as it bakes. The other option is to set the muffins in a 3 × 2 cup muffin tin and set the tin in the 12-inch Dutch oven. In my instructions, I describe the first option.

TOOLS

12-inch Dutch oven
12–14 coals below
20–24 coals above

INGREDIENTS

1 egg (2 Tbsp. egg powder + 3 Tbsp. water)
1 cup sugar
3/4 cup milk (mixed from powder)
1/2 cup vegetable oil (or reconstituted powdered shortening, or clarified butter)

3 tsp. baking powder
1/2 tsp. salt
1/2 tsp. ground nutmeg
1/4 tsp. ground cinnamon
1 cup all-purpose flour
1 cup rolled oats

1 cup raisins

THE FIRST thing I do when making muffins is to heat up the coals and get the Dutch oven preheating with coals below and above.

Then, I'll mix the first set of ingredients. I'll actually use a stiff whisk and get it as fluffy as I can. This will help aerate the batter and make it lift more while baking.

I'll mix the second set of ingredients together into a bowl. While continuing to whisk, I'll gradually add the powders to the wet ingredients until it's all nicely combined. Finally, I'll fold in the raisins.

In the prep area, I'll set out the metal cups and pour the batter in about ¾ of the way to the top of each. Then I'll lift the Dutch oven lid and carefully set as many of the cups onto the bottom of the Dutch oven as I can fit. Be careful, but work as quickly as possible. I'll close up the lid and mark the time.

They should be done in about 20 minutes, if the Dutch oven was properly preheated. Lift them out with tongs or gloves and let them cool. Then gobble them down!

RESOURCES

Ingredients and Supplies

http://www.thrivelife.com/

http://www.foodstoragedepot.com/

http://beprepared.com/

http://www.thereadystore.com/

https://www.lds.org/topics/food-storage

http://www.foodinsurance.com/

http://www.areyouprepared.com/

http://foodstorageguys.com/

http://canorganizer.com/

https://store.foodstoragemadeeasy.net/

http://www.survival-warehouse.com/

Advice

http://foodstoragemadeeasy.net/

https://www.lds.org/topics/food-storage

http://www.foodinsurance.com/

http://www.areyouprepared.com/

http://www.nutrition.gov/shopping-cooking-meal-planning/food-storage-and-preservation

http://thesurvivalmom.com/

http://www.peakprosperity.com/wiki/133/food-storage

http://eatingfoodstorage.blogspot.com/

http://www.preparedldsfamily.blogspot.com/

http://www.cookingwithmyfoodstorage.com/

http://foodstorage2.blogspot.com/

Dutch Oven

http://marksblackpot.com

http://dutchovenmadness.blogspot.com

http://idos.org

http://www.outdoor-cooking.com/

RECIPE INDEX

S

T

W

ABOUT THE AUTHOR

MARK STARTED cooking in his Dutch ovens in 2006, when his wife surprised him with one as a Father's Day present. His first cooking attempt was pizza, and the family instantly declared it a success! He began a tradition of cooking the family's Sunday dinners in his Dutch ovens.

In April of the following year, he thought he should start sharing what he learned, and he established the Mark's Black Pot blog. Years and hundreds of recipes later, it's still one of the most widely read Dutch oven blogs on the Internet.

Mark lives in Eagle Mountain, Utah, with his wife, Jodi, and two boys, who are also budding chefs.

0 26575 14832 9